S0-DTC-442

JUL 2 9 2004

THIS BOOK is an enduring memorial to the men, women, and children whose lives were lost in the tragic events of September 11, 2001. Support has been provided generously by Carnegie Corporation of New York.

THE BRANCH LIBRARIES

The New York Public Library
www.nypl.org

Fallback Position

Fallback Position

PREPARING A
CONTINGENCY PLAN
FOR THE
WORST CASE
SCENARIO

John E. Arnold

6021 SW 29th St. Suite A #267
Topeka, KS 66614
Phone: 785-273-1700   Toll Free: 866-385-1700
Fax: 785-228-2559   Email: info@exurba.com
www.exurba.com

Editor: Laren Bright
Cover & Interior Design: Peri Poloni, Knockout Design, www.knockoutbooks.com
Book Consultant: Ellen Reid, Smarketing

First Edition
Printed in the United States of America
ISBN 0-9729776-1-9
Library of Congress Control Number: 2003092430

Publisher's Cataloging-in-Publication
(Provided by Quality Books)

Arnold, John E.
    Anyone who can be fired needs a fallback position: preparing a contingency plan for the worst case scenario / John E. Arnold
    p. cm.
    Includes bibliographical references
    ISBN 0-9729776-1-9

    1. Unemployment—Psychological aspects. 2. Career changes—Psychological aspects. 3. Unemployed—Life skills guides I. Title.

HD5708.A76 2003   650.14
                                QBI33-1252

Article on 5 Coping Points from "Managing Your Career" Reprinted by permission from CareerJournal.com ©Dow Jones & Co. Inc. All rights reserved.

Article on "Money Management Tips for the Laid Off" reprinted by permission of the author, David Geller of GV Financial Advisors.

"After the Pink Slip" reprinted by permission from CareerJournal.com ©Dow Jones & Co. Inc. All rights reserved.

Article on "Job Road Mapping" from *Putting Your Best Foot Forward*, reprinted by permission of the author, Richard H. Hughes.

Quote from *Life Stratigies* by Phillip C. McGraw. Copyright ©1999 by Phillip C. McGraw, Ph.D. Reprinted by permission of Hyperion.

Fallback Position

❦

A BOOK FOR ANYONE

who can
be Fired at a Moment's Notice
by an Employer with the Potential
to be Completely Unfair, Unreasonable,
and Inconsiderate

for anyone who can be Down-sized,
Right-sized, Re-organized,
Re-invented, Re-engineered,
and Out-sourced
—without Warning,
by Bosses who are NOT thinking of you
and

THAT MEANS YOU!

John E. Arnold

This book is dedicated to my
wife, Kaye, our two sons,
Jay and L.T., and the lessons
they've each taught me.

John E. Arnold

———∞∞∞———

Whatever Happened to Job Security?!

The short answer is that, nowadays, you have to make it yourself. This is the book that tells you how.

Fallback Position is **the** "Plan B" guidebook for executives, managers, and any employee who can be fired at a moment's notice by an employer with the potential to be completely unfair, unreasonable and inconsiderate. It is required reading for anyone who can be down-sized, right-sized, re-organized, re-invented, re-engineered or outsourced without warning by bosses who are not thinking of you.

Thanks to *Fallback Position,* you will know that when you're told to pack up your office and be out in 30 minutes is not the time to be trying to negotiate your exit package. The time for that is when you are the fair-haired child being court-ed for the position. This is the kind of in-advance, Be Prepared thinking that keeps you in the driver's seat with your job and career. In addition to knowing exactly what you will do if the axe falls, you also have a deep peace of mind that helps you work better, putting you in the best position to be the last person let go when downsizing hits or the company goes belly up.

The one time John Arnold was fired, he was secure enough

to joke with a reporter, saying he was fired due to illness and fatigue: He was sick of the job and they were tired of him. It's that kind of breezy style that makes Fallback Position interesting and engaging. However, the light touch doesn't in any way dilute the sheer power of the information and exercises that pack these pages.

John Arnold's 30 years in the public and private sector have provided him with the experience to know the ropes and not get tangled in them. His native wit and intelligence give him the ability to catalog what he learned and communicate it clearly so everyone who doesn't own their company—and their families—can benefit.

In today's volatile work environment, this is the book that can calm the sea of uncertainty and help every employee sleep better at night knowing they are ready for whatever happens in the morning. It really is true: Everyone needs a *Fallback Position!*

J<!-- -->**ohn E. Arnold** is an expert on leadership, management, and financial subjects. He writes with humor and compassion from a rock solid foundation of thirty years experience ranging from employee to manager of nine organizations with workers numbering 75 to 1300. He has reported to 200 different board members and 25 different chairpeople, has seen good management and bad, and he knows employees need to be protected from the latter. His books are geared to helping employees, and others, prosper in the workplace and in their private lives. John lives in Topeka, Kansas and writes, speaks and consults on work and financial issues, leadership, motivation, creativity, and the future.

Table of Contents

———∞∞∞———

Prologue 13

CHAPTER 1.   When to Say: "They Can't Do That!" 29

CHAPTER 2.   Things I've Always Wanted to Do 65

CHAPTER 3.   Things to Do Right Away if You're Fired: *Financial* 77

CHAPTER 4.   Financial Specifics 115

CHAPTER 5.   Things to Do Right Away in Your Profession 129

CHAPTER 6.   Things to Do Right Away if You're Fired: *Personal* 139

CHAPTER 7.   The Likelihood of You Being Fired in a Career 161

CHAPTER 8.   Life is Self-Correcting 165

CHAPTER 9.   Appendices 189
              Suggested Further Readings
              Sample Employment Agreement
              Sample Termination Agreement
              Acknowlegments
              Experience John Arnold

HERMAN®

5-19　　　　　　　　　　　　　　　　　© 1986 Jim Unger

**"I'm not interested in excuses.
You're four minutes late."**

The *Fallback Position* is Applicable to You!

This is a book for those who are in danger of being moved out of a job for whatever reason, under whatever euphemism the organization uses, whether that organization is private, public, or non-profit and whether the position is the CEO, the Manager, the Executive Director, the Superintendent, the Department Head, the Division Head, or any other position. The information applies to you.

I have worked for public and non-profit agencies and have been a consultant in the private sector. My network of experienced practitioners in all sectors has helped make this information applicable to all. I come from a career background that was mostly public, with the hiring authority being an elected city council, a group that often has no management, supervisory, hiring, or firing experience whatsoever. That can be better than being dependent on pleasing a single CEO or supervisor, or it can be worse. But having hired dozens of employees and fired a few, and having spent a career watching others hire and fire and being hired and fired, I've learned a lot about how it all happens.

For purposes of convenience, the governing body will be

used in place of the various words for hiring authorities, whether that be a Board of Directors, a City Council, or even a CEO. The point is that the entity or person to whom you owe your position is the potential threat. It's been said, "You're hired by your friends, but that's not who lets you go."

If you're prepared, being fired can actually be useful to you. If you're not prepared, it can be more traumatic than you can imagine. So the Boy Scout motto to "Be Prepared" applies here.

Don't just take my word that being fired can be useful, and that preparing for it well in advance can be even more beneficial than harmful. Here's an article from the **Wall Street Journal's** career advice website, called www.CareerJournal.com, that speaks to the issue.

AFTER THE PINK SLIP: FORMULATE A GAME PLAN

By Eugene Raudsepp

"Being fired" is a phrase most of us don't like to use. We prefer euphemisms: Discharged, dismissed, terminated, retired early, separated, laid-off, furloughed, eased out, outplaced, or even resigned.

Incompetence and performance problems aren't the primary reasons people are let go. The usual causes range from staff reductions, mergers and changes in corporate direction to personality clashes, political conflicts and bad chemistry with the boss. Sometimes, however, firing does reflect personal failure: A person doesn't perform up to standards; is habitually late to work; has excessive absenteeism; takes excessively long lunch hours; has cost the company business or failed to bring in new business; or has failed to conform to a company's way of doing things.

Whatever the reason, getting fired can be one of life's most stressful experiences. The higher you are in the corporate structure, the greater the harrowing impact.

The first reactions to being fired are usually anger and pain, followed by feelings of confusion and disillusionment. Unless these feelings are aired out with a friend or counselor, your self-esteem becomes shaky. You're overwhelmed by a crippling sensation of powerlessness, depression and fear.

For some, the shock of being let go produces a psychological numbness. But whether they feel numb or depressed, these states of mind strain the energy needed to launch a job search.

Many laid-off people start sleeping late or watching television endlessly. Some comfort themselves with solitary pleasures like reading and walking. Ashamed, they avoid friends, or assume friends are avoiding them. Their relationships with their immediate families also suffer as they grow defensive, cynical and bitter. Often they reach complete despair before the self-healing process takes over and they can get back on track again.

While no one likes to be moved out of the mainstream into the backwater of surplus people, some navigate unemployment with relative ease. They stay out of a self-defeating rut by immediately seeking the help of friends or a therapist to convert feelings of frustration, anger and loss into positive energy and action. They attend professional meetings, take skill-building evening courses, attend career workshops, study and respond to recruitment ads, read magazines and newsletters in their fields, maintain a wide network of contacts, and use a variety of other resources to focus their job searches. These people maintain a confident and in-charge attitude, enabling them to land new jobs in a few months.

A WELL-DISGUISED BLESSING

While getting laid off isn't a boon for a career, it can be a positive experience. If you use the break for self-improvement instead of self-pity, you can emerge a winner. Yet few people view termination as an opportunity to lay a foundation for future career satisfaction.

When you're unemployed, you have a chance to explore new careers and fields, find a better fitting job, or perhaps even start your own business. An enforced sabbatical provides an excellent opportunity for self-rediscovery. Who are you? Why do you do what you do? What do you really want to do?

This opportunity to mull things over lets you rediscover your values and goals — or at least pry them loose for examination and reassessment. A restorative break helps you put your true concerns — the things that are really relevant to you — into sharper focus.

Many people fall into jobs or seize available openings rather than plan their careers. Little wonder their work isn't properly matched to their interests, skills and personalities.

Others find themselves in energy-draining jobs that leave them demoralized and exhausted. Still others work in jobs where they're unappreciated, undervalued and swamped with unchallenging and burdensome duties.

A career examination period gives you the chance to correct a bad job choice. It can free you from a situation in which you felt used or used up. It can help you break out of a holding pattern that offers no further growth prospects.

When the boss calls you into his office and says, "We're going to have to let you go," you might be tempted to tell him off or threaten revenge. Don't. It's the worst thing you can do. In return, he might give you a terrible reference or find other means to undercut your attempts to find a new job.

The best way to leave is gracefully and with dignity. Chances are the boss and company feel guilty about your termination and will be glad to give you solid references, a generous severance package and outplacement counseling. They may even supply you with helpful contacts. Furthermore, should your career paths cross in the future, your self-control and cool demeanor won't be forgotten.

If you can maintain your cool, you're in a position to negotiate a better severance package and, depending on company policy, a few weeks of time and office space. This will allow you to keep your contacts and friendships with your associates and tap them for any job leads. Co-workers often are more than willing to help you, especially during the first few weeks after your dismissal.

The first few days after a termination are crucial and should be devoted to carefully examining your situation.

Many people feel panicky and call their associates and search firms immediately. Feeling angry and confused, they come across poorly and often scare people off.

To avoid such self-defeating behavior, accept and examine your emotions. Share them with someone who is understanding, friendly and supportive. Don't bottle up resentment or self-pity; such feelings inevitably get transmitted in any future job-interview situation, whether the interview occurs two months or six months after termination. No prospective employer is impressed with someone who has a chip on his shoulder or wallows in self-pity.

By talking to someone who is unconditionally supportive, you free yourself of all negative emotions and feelings. It helps draw a curtain over the past, allowing you to face the future more confidently.

When you've been fired, try to negotiate enough severance pay to cover the time it usually takes someone of your level and skill to find a new job. Some companies provide one week's to one month's pay for each year of employment. Many companies have been known to extend severance payments a month or two beyond the formal limit, if you take your severance in regular paychecks rather than in a lump sum.

You also should arrange for continuation of your health and life insurance coverage until you can find a new job. Under the Consolidated Omnibus Budget Reconciliation Act (COBRA), employers are required to make health coverage available for up to 18 months for terminated employees. Find out if you can convert your policy to an individual policy with no lapse in coverage.

Make sure you extract a promise of decent references and job-search help from an outplacement firm. Outplacement assistance used to be provided only for top executives, but now is offered to middle managers or executives and technical professionals as well.

Finally, make a thorough analysis of your finances and liquid assets. Add up your basic cost-of-living outlays and fixed expenses: mortgage, rent, utilities, etc. Next, add up your available assets and sources of income: severance pay, unemployment compensation (don't be too proud to collect it), interest and dividends on investments and your spouse's income. Then revise your budget according to a realistic assessment of how much time it might take you to find another job. Don't make any major purchases or take expensive vacations, and avoid borrowing unnecessarily or extending your credit lines. Simply adopt a more modest lifestyle — without overdoing it.

— From the archives of the *National Business Employment Weekly*. The late Mr. Raudsepp, who was president of Princeton Creative Research Inc., a Princeton, N.J., consulting firm, was a frequent NBEW contributor between 1984 and 1995. This article was selected for its continuing relevance.

The Game Plan is the Fallback Position. That's what this book is about: Helping you to form that game plan and prepare that fallback position, so you actually prosper through the change.

HERMAN®

4-22   © 1982 Jim Unger

"Did you fire Williams in
'Fruit & Vegetables'?"

Expect the Best but Prepare for the Worst

You have to learn from the mistakes of others.
You won't live long enough to make them all yourself.

—Anonymous

⎯oreo⎯

I t has occurred to me from time to time, as I have sat in governing body meetings with the occasional harangue of one member by another, that the people to whom I owe some allegiance are not always the most considerate and humane of individuals. Sometimes I have witnessed even what others would have judged as inappropriate behavior of one human toward another. These are the people to whom I have temporarily pledged my troth, professionally speaking.

I have even heard stories about my compatriots being fired. More frequently, though, the opportunity to resign is offered, by an individual or by a board, when the votes for dismissal are there. And as former manager Ray Wells said, "Every time a majority of the governing body gets together for coffee, one of the items on the agenda is whether the votes are there." It's the same with the single supervisor—every time there's an interaction, a transaction of business, between you and your hiring authority, the question in his or her mind is, "Does this person contribute enough value to the organization to continue the relationship?" That question may be unspoken or even unconscious, but it's there.

When I began writing this book, I had never been fired. But just before it was published, I was fired. Technically my contract was just cancelled. But it felt like a firing, and, as they say, "If it walks like a duck and talks like a duck, it is a duck." So if it feels like firing, newspapers report it as a firing, etc., it is a firing. It really doesn't matter to anyone but me, I guess, but what matters for this discussion is that I have contemplated the guillotine from below and so know the tightness of the neck muscles which occurs.

It's also apparent that it is becoming easier for the odd member of the governing body to line up the votes and dismiss the executive. Boards are becoming less and less inclined to tolerate the manager who doesn't fit hand and glove the philosophical bent of the current majority. And there isn't as much latitude or time given to the new executive to make the organization adjust to the new approach, or for the executive to adjust. Then too, there is a fair amount of board turnover and that creates additional tension, as still more adjustments are needed all around.

I would be remiss if I didn't mention the news coverage of the likes of Al "Chainsaw" Dunlap, the so-called "Turnaround CEO" who comes into an organization and immediately announces a layoff of 10,000 employees, watching the stock price rise as a result, capturing nice stock option bonuses on the bodies of the unemployed. We all hope we never have to work in an organization that hires such "one-trick ponies", but it does happen. Enron, WorldCom, Tyco, Adelphia—the news is rife with examples where executives pillaged the company for their own benefit and rode right over the bodies of the employees, some like Enron executives, saying, "Keep your Enron Stock in your 401 (k)," while in their own accounts they were selling.

Of course, the dot-com bubble bursting beginning in March of 2000 cost many thousands of people their jobs. And many thousands more their retirement security and assets. In some cases these companies had solid products and good prospects, but got caught in the melt-down of the technology sector. In others, the business plan was flawed from the start, but it looked good enough to the investment bankers, and the lure of the Initial Public Offering running up the price of a speculative stock providing wealth for all was too much to resist. Many employees got caught in that snare.

After 9-11-01 many companies with leadership that had integrity had some difficulty. Many laid off thousands of employees not due to mismanagement, but due to massive change in society. Those kinds of changes can occur in any industry, at any time. And they are unpredictable, so most people are unprepared for them.

So having heard people talk about the phenomenon, having watched it occur throughout society, and having experienced some of it, I thought it might be useful to try to put into writing some of what I have learned over the years, directly and from others, about preparing for the eventuality of separation before another job is lined up. That's an important point, because having another job lined up is a promotion or a new career, and those are explicitly positive moves that feed the ego and strengthen the psyche.

This is about the other side of the coin, the occasion when the separation is not a desired or a timely one for the individual.

So the purpose of this book is to describe how to prepare for the time when that untimely separation might occur. The intent is to give readers things to think about and prepare for, things that will enable them to handle the event more easily and, more than that, help them cope with the worst part of the event—the fear that precedes it immediately before it happens.

(This guide doesn't work for the private sector executive who appoints his own board, paying each a retainer of $70,000 a year with 4,000 stock options. That executive is not very responsive to the governing body and the board doesn't offer much in the way of supervision or criticism. The executive has to get into severe trouble (as an Enron or Arthur Anderson)—with a governing body that has to act—before they will. Even so, they provide the shiniest of golden parachutes. One of the best I've heard is that of Westar's David Wittig, as reported in the *Topeka Capital Journal*: If he's fired he gets his salary for 17 years and all the money he's spent on his house is refunded plus 17%. It's no coincidence that he bought a most expensive house and is spending $1.5 million remodeling it. He's reported to be a whiz at math, but it doesn't take one to figure out that's a heckuva deal. His deal is figured at somewhere between $55 and $101 million. We could all have a safe landing with that parachute.)

Fallback Position is quite simply a guide for normal people. It's a manual for coping, an instruction book on personal emergency preparedness, and a resource that allows you to create your own support system, your own contingency plan, for the worst-case scenario.

Fallback Position also provides you with the tools to help avoid being fired. That is, it doesn't tell you how to deal with a difficult governing body, a difficult supervisor, or a difficult situation. It does, however, provide you with the tools to build your own fallback position and, in so doing, gives you confidence that you needn't worry about or fear the event. The tool that eliminates fear is probably the single most important one in your kit bag for dealing with difficult situations or people to the best of your ability. If you know what you're going to do, financially, personally, and with your family, and you know you'll be okay and they'll be okay, then you can deal with the difficult people with equanimity. Chances are that this will enhance others' esteem for you and help solve any problem the supervisor perceives, increasing your value and longevity on the job.

In short, *Fallback Position* is like insurance. Just having it in place may help you avoid needing it.

What the *Fallback Position* does is provide information about the most common and the most obscure of concerns an employee has, and answer some questions that usually aren't even thought of until the disaster occurs. For example, is a manager who is fired eligible for unemployment compensation after the severance package expires? Is it the same answer if the manager resigns? (The answer is, It depends on how it was done and what the termination documents say. And it's important for the manager or executive to know that.)

Not that an executive is going to run out and apply for unemployment. Most would rather not, seeing unemployment as some sort of welfare that a respectable executive would not accept. But we're talking about a fallback position here, and we're talking about disaster preparedness. So let's say an executive hasn't found a job in twelve months and she's faced with significant changes in lifestyle for her family. She needs to know the eligibility requirements at the time she's working out details of the separation, not 12 months later.

Granted, the executive in Wittig's case doesn't have to think about unemployment compensation, and the amount provided by unemployment won't keep anyone living in the style to which they've become accustomed. It's just that it is one of the factors of the financial options that need to be understood by most people facing job loss.

This book attempts to provide the reader with a set of tools that, if used correctly, will provide a fallback position. (In military strategic terms, a fallback position is a place where you can be comfortable for a time when retreat is called for.) From there one can regain spirit, regroup, and live to fight again.

At the same time, it is intended to provide some light-hearted guidance to what truly is a period of severe difficulty. As Harlan Cleveland advises, after a lifetime of witnessing the tragedy and trial of American government: "What people laugh at is always a serviceable index to what troubles them most deeply." He illustrates that by summarizing a brief career in the State Department as saying, "There, no one signs anything they write nor writes anything they sign." There is no question that the security of most managerial positions in the world of today troubles practitioners deeply. But they laugh about it. They have to.

*"Lord, give me the strength
to keep out of other people's business."*
—Monty Johnson

DISCLAIMER

Any document purporting to offer advice, mostly on things that are practical, but somewhat on things legal and on things tax accountable, has to acknowledge that it will not fit for everyone and that the legal comments are not legal advice, nor are the tax comments tax advice. The reader must get his or her own professional advice in these technical matters. But the guide does offer some suggested areas in which to go hunting advice.

We all know it's easier to get the right answer from the specialists and attorneys if the right question is asked, and this document attempts to provide the reader with the knowledge of the right questions to ask the experts.

HERMAN®

"That guy who's filling in for you at the
office is a real hard worker."

CHAPTER 1

When to Say: "They Can't Do That!"

*"I don't know who won it, but if we had lost
I know who would have been blamed."*

—Gen. Joseph Joffre,
French General upon winning the Battle of the Marne

———∞∞∞———

We all think we will know when it is time to go, and we'll know it well before it happens. But many of our friends and colleagues—knowledgeable and sensitive folks all—have been surprised by a cabal of supervisors or a boss acting precipitously.

I've calculated I've worked with and for 200 city council members and 25 Mayors. As my friend Bill Morgan, former President of Colorado State University, said, "God will grant special dispensation from purgatory for such service."

Several of those I worked with would have loved to have been able to say they "got rid of Arnold." A few did when I moved on. But several were basically unhealthy personalities. One was particularly so. So much so, a fellow councilmember said that guy was "certifiable." Another heard that comment and said, "No, he's not crazy enough to be committed; but if he was *in*, they wouldn't let him *out*." This was a councilmember who made a motion in council to "get another city manager", and couldn't get a second to his motion from the other members. Since there were fourteen other council members, it was a bit of a victory for me. But there is always someone out there with a maverick viewpoint. And there is often someone who wants to take advantage, to gain power, or maybe just indulge their ego because they "got the big guy." (Almost anyone is in danger of being fired by someone whose ego is so weak that demonstrating the power of termination makes him feel superior. You don't even have to be a "big guy" in order to feed that ego.)

On a couple of occasions I've worked for folks who seemed to need the ego stroking of power; the relationship became dysfunctional, and I've had to draw a line in the sand, marking a place beyond which I could not go or a place beyond which, if they went, then *I* would go.

I've believed strongly in service of the democratic process by helping the elected officials do their thing, whatever the light as they saw it defined their thing. And I've been willing to compromise if I disagreed. Within limits of morality, legality, and some modicum of good sense, I've done so. But elected officials and other supervisors can get messed up.

We've all heard of the governing body which demands that "two department heads be fired or you are." Then, the manager has to choose between his or her value system and the job, or to decide between his or her success on this job or just *holding* onto the job. While that kind of thing occurs only occasionally, it's still useful for any employee to have a game plan in mind.

The more that game plan includes defining what the employee will not tolerate, the better.

Some people would soften that approach: One said, "You have no responsibility to be thrown out the door." Action in such a situation is not universal. I just figure that if I'm an employee of any organization, I want to be treated by the hiring authority or boss on the basis of my performance, not on some personal or political whim. Every organization can be humane in the way it treats its people, and every one should be. The easiest way to ensure the organization is humane is to apply the Golden Rule in all policies dealing with people: Treat them as you would be treated.

THE FALLBACK POSITION
IS A FUTURES EXERCISE

In one sense *Fallback Position* is just a personal extension of professional futures planning. As a manager or employee of whatever business or entity, you are constantly looking at trends and forecasting from them. You make inferences about the future from these trends. The activity of personal planning is similar. You, as an individual, are always looking around, trying to figure out what's going on, to avoid being behind the curve on trends. This is an informal strategic planning process, the SWOT analysis: Strengths, Weaknesses, Opportunities, and Threats.

Of course, any adult looks to his or her future financial situation, to provide for the education of children, care of parents, retirement costs, and disposition of estate.

Just as you would use "what-if" scenarios in professional futures planning and personal financial planning, you will do best to have a fallback plan for the worst-case professional scenario.

But what I'm proposing is more than that. It can make the difference between initial depression and genuine anticipation. This is not to suggest the approach is a panacea. After all, getting fired, no matter what formal, official euphemism is used, is still a shock. It's the same kind of shock to the system as being dumped when in your teens by the love of your life. Your ego is damaged. Others don't see you for the marvel that you are. Maybe some think you weren't as good as they thought (or so you perceive). There are even people who think you did something wrong, whether illegal, immoral, or just dumb. When you're fired, people talk to your spouse, your kids, and other staff. They say these things. It's all stressful.

I believe the stress is the same whether you are fired or gently nudged to move on. If the majority of the governing body has the votes to move you on before you judge it the right time, or if you work for one individual and he or she is not happy with you, you will suffer a similar level of stress.

Some have characterized the stress akin to the grief of death. Magruder called it "a little death," wherein the same stages are passed through as in the surprise death of a loved one, or in the approach of your own death, as listed by Kubler-Ross: Denial, Anger, Bargaining, Depression, Acceptance.

The period of grieving moves us through those stages. A fallback plan is really needed during the first two phases; the plan helps you get through those quickly and positively, until you are able to cope and get on with your life.

START WITH "WHO AM I?"

It's important to know who we are. We like who we are,

most of the time, and we don't spend much time thinking about it. Oh, we did when we were teen-agers and when we were in college trying to "find ourselves," but since then we've pretty well settled into something that relates to self-knowledge. It might be what the late Dr. Kenneth Boulding referred to as his "image" of knowledge, his subjective world-view that guides his actions. We all, I expect, are guided by how we perceive the world and ourselves.

Personal life planning, as part of a total, holistic approach to self-improvement, is a valuable program for defining who you are, for defining your values. Many exercises have been developed to allow us to better think about who we are and how to guide our life around that conclusion. One such is called *The Obituary*. It's simple: List the top ten things you would like to have listed in your obituary; these are the things you would like most to be remembered for.

(This is to be distinguished from the Epitaph, which is the message, the sometimes witty phrase found on tombstones. You recall W.C. Fields' apocryphal epitaph: "On the whole, I'd rather be in Philadelphia." Or "I told you I was sick." Or "Died at 97, Suffering Illness All Her Days.")

This is the Obituary, the summary of the life. Some newspapers allow loved ones to write obits for the dearly departed; those tend to get a bit lengthy and sometimes maudlin. Most papers have beginning journalists spend months writing obits because the ability to summarize a life in a few paragraphs is good training for how to cover the news concisely.

Now in thinking about the list in your Obit, you would exclude the things you would put on a resume. After all, obit time isn't the time to be qualifying for another job—it's time to list the things that are truly important. The immortal items: real values; things you'd like your great-grandchildren to know.

So you make your own list now. The Top Ten list of *What's Most Important to Me*. Things for which you'd like to be remembered:

1. _____

2. _____

3. _____

4. _____

5. _____

6. _____

7. _____

8. _____

9. _____

10. _____

Did you put down the things you like to do, with your skills noted: Basketball player—and could dunk? Golfer who beats her or his handicap when playing for money? Green Bay Packer Couch Potato with an unbroken record? Duck hunter, fisherman, jogger, writer, gourmet cook?

Or did you put down some of the things on which you spend your time: Rotarian with unbroken attendance for 30 years? Member of 17 community organizations and committees that bettered the city?

WHEN TO GO: "THEY CAN'T DO THAT!'"   35

Or did you list those things you gave your money to: Tithed at Church for twenty years? Supported an orphan in the Philippines? Built the University Fund by contributing annually at the Patron level? United Way supporter? Sustaining Member of the Symphony?

Now this is not to be confused with Bumper Sticker Philosophy. Of the thousands of things to be in support of, some people will select a few to espouse on their bumper stickers. I always have a problem with that. Which causes do I favor enough to list over all the others? You see an old Honda with a sticker that says, "Teach Peace" and another sticker that says "No Off-shore Oil Wells", shown by the circle/slash oil derrick symbol. Then the car has a sticker for the public education radio station. But no National Rifle Association sticker.

I saw a car once with the all-time record—27 bumper stickers. As I stood on the sidewalk counting and reading them all, the driver came out and I complimented her: Told her she got the award for the most bumper stickers—and the most complex set of values I'd ever seen. She was pumped up and pleased. (I didn't tell her the multiple values shown appeared to me to be more confused than just complex. I didn't need to start some new kind of road rage, maybe called "bumper sticker rage.")

When it comes to bumper stickers, I like the bumper sticker that cites the current cynical political philosophy: "Two Terms: One in Office. One in jail." Or the one the late columnist Herb Caen of the **San Francisco Chronicle** noted: "Horn Broke: Watch for Finger!"

The Obituary, however, is not bumper sticker philosophy.

It clearly is a value exercise. What role is most important to you? If you're like most people you'll have a list that includes Father, Husband, Son, Brother (for men, of course), Christian (or Jew or Baptist or Muslim, etc.), maybe Citizen, Friend, and then follows maybe occupation, maybe a hobby that you do well, (musician, poet, cook, golfer, or woodworker). Everyone's list is different, but most have the similarity that the occupation is a good deal farther down the list than each of us would have thought.

That's useful when you sit at a meeting and things aren't going your way. You start to feel the pressure that others might think you're not doing the job well, that you're not doing it the way you should, that someone is fussing at you, that you should be stronger, that...**they can't do that**!

It's useful in that circumstance to remember your list of what's important to you. It's your value system, not someone else's. It's what is important to you that counts, not what's important to someone else—even if it is the governing body or your individual supervisor.

And that's the essence of a fallback position.

NEXT: "WHAT AM I FOR?"

"It's often easier to fight for one's principles
than to live up to them."
—Adlai Stevenson

⸺⸺

Add to that list another Top 10 list: What Am I For? What are the known values I hold? These are things I really believe in, are important, and that are worthy of going to battle for.

Make yourself another list:

1. _____

2. _____

3. _____

4. _____

5. _____

6. _____

7. _____

8. _____

9. _____

10. _____

These are items like honesty in all things, human rights, integrity, the right to bear arms, the right to free choice, belief in my country and my government, the right of the elected official to be treated as if exalted by the election process. The knowledge that the democratic process works in the long-run, though it might be flawed when looked at from one council meeting night to the next, and it might be flawed from one election to the next or to the next several. Take comfort in the knowledge that it works in the long-run. But don't fret about one week to the next.

In the non-profit sector the things you are for might be volunteerism and community participation as the essence of community. It might be helping the less fortunate, who can't help themselves, helping to provide a social safety net. It might be both, as support and involvement with the United Way.

In the for-profit sector it might be supporting the capitalist system. It might be the opportunity to acquire wealth. It might be supporting the Generally Accepted Accounting Practices for honesty in transactions and protecting stockholders. Avoiding Enron kinds of debacles would be surely supportive. It might be an understanding that the capitalist system is what makes the democratic process work best. That the capitalist system supports individual freedom more than anything else and is in fact essential to that freedom.

Your list of things you are for might also be like support for the community, the quality of life, the involvement of the people in things that affect them, the public's right to know, support for the citizen as an individual, a strong public education system, maybe even free education through college.

There are also things like support for the institution, loyalty to your supervisor, and helping them make the right decision in the right way. Support for the staff and not leaving them hanging out, "spinning in the wind" as the Nixon-era tapes described some staff taking the fall.

If you're a Board member or in a management position and are struggling with the new changes in ethics and board or corporate responsibilities, it might be trying to find the common ground between support and accountability. Support for the staff and accountability to the stockholders. It might be creating value for the stockholder, creating jobs for the employees, allowing the economy to expand, and ratcheting throughout society.

In any position it might also be support for the Constitution and the Bill of Rights and perhaps for social equity. Maybe it's for the American Way of Life, as you define it. And it might be support for law and good order and maybe for a private economy.

This list is for the more abstract values you hold. It may or may not have anything to do with your job. But it helps you define what is important, and in so doing to prepare yourself the ultimate fallback position.

The combination of personal desires and values is what Stephen Covey talks about in **_The Seven Habits of Highly Effective People_**, a topically important book. He describes one of the seven habits as the things you want to be remembered for. "Begin with the end in mind," he says. "Think how you want to be remembered at your funeral, and then act accordingly everyday."

CROSS-OVER LINE

> *"It's better to have a bad plan*
> *than to have no plan at all":*
> **_—Charles De Gaulle_**

Both of the Top 10 lists you have made are mental exercises that allow you to define your fallback position. That is, you will know just how far you can fallback and just how far you will go in working with others before you will go no more. This is the Cross-Over Line: Beyond here if they go, then I go.

The ancient map-makers identified the unknown areas by writing, "Beyond Here There Be Dragons." You need to know where that boundary line is, and it's different for everyone. It's individual.

That line should not be drawn haphazardly or cavalierly. It is a serious business that speaks eloquently of your values. And it cannot be used as a threat; in fact, until it is crossed it cannot be used in communication. It's not like a "Doomsday Machina," that is only useful if both sides know it exists and each is killed by the actions of the other. It's purely your own "line in the sand" that defines the boundary beyond which you will not go. It's good for you to know that you know where it is, and can recognize when it has been crossed.

Once you have defined who you are and what you are for, the line beyond which you cannot go is much less troublesome to you. You know what is important and why.

It should be added, though, that the cross-over line is one that changes with time and with different experiences. Dr. John Nalbandian of the University of Kansas suggests that "learning from experience" may be defined as the "ability to redraw the line." Then the metaphor of the line in the sand as a place beyond which you will not go is useful as a changing place, because a line in the sand disappears over time as the winds blow and the sand shifts. Remember, though, what Will Rogers said about learning from experience. He said "Good judgment comes from experience, and most experience comes from bad judgment." So we learn by doing. And maybe more by doing it wrongly.

FOXHOLE COMPANION SCALE

"Cover me..." —***John Wayne***

Everyone needs support from someone. And any executive needs some level of support from the hiring authority. Of course there is support from staff, usually, and from spouse, usually, and from friends. That's personal support. The most essential. But the chief level of professional support must come from the boss, whether that's a governing body or an individual. That is, that person or group who brought you to the dance is the one you need to dance with most. Over time, these folks change and it becomes necessary to develop relationships with new folks; it then gets to be a choice whether to dance with them or not. But an executive by whatever title always needs to have a majority that she or he would like to dance with.

At my advanced age, I figure I can get along with any kind of board member more or less, but I judge them on the scale of approbation I call the Foxhole Companion Scale. They can be for anything they want, but a good board member is one you would be comfortable with in a foxhole in a shooting war. They watch your back while you watch theirs. No one has the fear of attack from within the foxhole.

I've only had a few I wouldn't want to be in a foxhole with, but those few are memorable.

One method I use to evaluate governing body members and whether I think they'll watch my back like I'll watch theirs is what I call The Foxhole Scale.

The scale runs from 1 to 10, from "Not in My Foxhole" to "I'm With You, Buddy".

1	2	3	4	5	6	7	8	9	10

Not in My Foxhole   **I'm With You, Buddy**

It's important to know whom you can trust, and to convey to the governing body that they can trust you. Humor is a good tool to use in addressing the question: it enhances understanding. A lack of mutual support in the board-executive relationship is probably what troubles executives most deeply. Boards too.

The non-profit sector has the same problem. The for-profit not so much, but occasionally so. Performance is generally easy to assess in the for-profit sector and if it's not there, it's easily communicated that it needs to be there or changes will be made. In the public and non-profit sector, the equation has more variables and is not as easy to evaluate.

DIFFERENCE BETWEEN PUBLIC AND PRIVATE

Roy Pederson, the former city manager of Scottsdale, Arizona, tells the story of hiring a deputy from the private sector, and asking her to let him know when she had figured out the difference between the way the private sector works and the way the public sector works. She came back after just a couple of months and said, "The differences are two: One, in the private sector you can do whatever is not prohibited by law, but in the public sector you can only do what is specifically authorized by law; and Two, the difference in the public sector and the private sector is that in the private sector there's never any question that the Board of Directors and Management are on the same side."

As we watched the melt-down of Enron, WorldCom, Arthur Andersen, Westar and more, it became clear the Board of Directors was not functioning as any kind of check on the excesses of management. So the Board was with management and in sync—on the same side. But the problem was that while the Board and the Administration were on the same side and working together, they didn't give a fig for the stockholder, the owner of the corporation, the investor, or the employee.

As a result of these lapses, there is great momentum to change these private boards. Private boards are becoming more like public bodies, in that they are becoming more accountable, more ethical, and more concerned with the interests of the public and the shareholders and becoming more transparent, something public boards have always been, mostly.

In my first job as a city manager, the state law prohibited any kind of closed meeting. Negotiation strategies for labor contracts were to be decided in public, amounts to offer in purchasing real estate were decided in public, and evaluation of the city manager was done in public. At the first of the evaluations, the fourteen councilmembers were nearly universally supportive and complimentary. One used the word, "Brilliant"—a bit over the top. Many other flattering things were said. It was just as stressful as if they were giving me hell or saying I'd performed badly. As a friend said, "Only your mother would believe all those things. Your employees won't, your staff won't, your wife and your kids won't. Just your mother."

Once, during an evaluation session in which the city council was trying to get me to commit to stay in another city for a long time, we were working some kinks out together. I offered to move on down the road if my philosophy no longer fit with the community. When three of the seven later thought that was a good idea, one councilmember who had been mayor decided to go along with them, because, as he told me, "some night I might come in mad at you and then vote to fire you, so I thought it would be better to vote with them now rather than later."

Not in my foxhole.

(This particular councilmember had been mayor the year the newspaper did a power and influence study of the community. It was a Top 10 list of those with "the juice." But exactly who was on the list was not revealed until each day a new profile was released, starting with Number 10. When they told me I was on the list, I thought this might not be healthy for my relationship with the governing body. I could only hope I was Number 10 and not higher. When 10 came and went and it wasn't me, I began to worry. Then 9 and it wasn't me either. When Number 8 popped up as the Mayor, I knew I was screwed. That meant I was going to be listed higher than he was, he would be ticked, and he'd never forget it. I turned out to be Number 3. And I was right about his thoughts and memory. He was the one who, two years later, came in and said he might be mad some night and vote against me. No surprise.)

WORRY QUOTIENT

"When you come to a fork in the road—take it":
—Yogi Berra

People have a set capacity for worry, and no matter their job or their situation, they will worry to that capacity. That's why the rich worry about their money: They worried about it when they didn't have it; they worried about it so much they worked hard to get it; now that they have it, they continue to worry to their capacity. So it doesn't matter where you are or what you're doing, you are likely to worry to your current level—unless you do something to change your level, and then I'm not sure you can. It's probably genetic. But just in case it is environmental, it probably is worth your time to try and change your worry level. Doing the exercises in this book is one way to help you accomplish that.

Clearly, it is not easy. And just as clearly I cannot convince you that it can be done. You've already started worrying about that, to whatever level you need to worry about it. "Will this book be a waste of time if it can't be guaranteed to help me?" you may be asking at this point. Or perhaps you're thinking, "It's not time to worry about it, but it might help." Maybe you are asking yourself, "Worry about what?" Worry is individual.

The first step in any problem solving is defining the problem. So if part of your problem is your worry quotient, then having recognized that fact puts you on the road to the solution. Many psychologists say as a way to deal with worry, "Find out what keeps you awake at night and solve that problem."

Stress is largely self-induced. I know many executives believe that's not true, that governing body members are stressors. And so are staff. But as one staffer said, "Governing body members don't *cause* the disease; they are only *carriers*." Stressors are also events: Disasters, disturbances, even societal changes. They are contributors. Jack Welch said of General Electric's many enterprises: "If we can't be #1 or #2 in each activity we shouldn't be in it at all." In the private sector competition is the main stressor. But stress still involves internalizing the problems as if you are the only one concerned and the only one to be faulted if the problem isn't solved.

This is not intended to treat stress cavalierly. But recognition of your own level of tolerance for ambiguity helps deal with the stress you will experience. An event occurring a second time doesn't cause as much stress as the first, the third less than the second, and so on. Then too, one type of event doesn't cause the same level of stress in everyone; stress is personal.

But we can also learn something about stress from James Bond's creator, Ian Fleming. He wrote James' method of paying attention and being concerned. The first occurrence of something endangering him, like he's jogging and a boulder comes crashing down the hill just missing him. He called that "Happenstance." The second time while he's jogging and a car careens around a corner and just misses him as he leaps into the ditch to avoid it, he called "Coincidence." But the third time a similar endangerment occurred, the tree fell near him, he called, "Planned Enemy Action." He acted accordingly.

So should a manager. Or any employee.

A FALLBACK POSITION

"The faster you go, the more you have to be ahead of the power curve":
—Fighter Pilot

———⊗∞⊗———

One way of looking at a fallback position is in the military sense. The dictionary says it is a "place to which a military unit retreats if the plans don't work out, a place in which the wounds are licked and the next engagement details are decided."

Another way of looking at a fallback position is in being prepared for the unpleasant and the unexpected.

It's like being CEO in a Board Meeting when you are asked a question by a Board Member to which you don't know the answer. There are several possible immediate fallback positions:

1. **You can respond by saying,**

   "As Charles Shultz' comic character Peppermint Patty says, in answer to the teacher's questions, for which she is unprepared, 'There are two kinds of people in the world, those who ask the questions and those who provide the answers. It's better to be one of those who asks the questions.'" That's probably acceptable for light questions or obtuse ones, when you have a good relationship with the supervisor and they know it's your sense of humor showing. Otherwise, it's probably not a good idea.

2. **You can respond by saying,**

   "I don't know the answer to that question, but I will find out, get back to you, and know the answer the next time. Or, if you prefer, we'll ask other staff members who are here if one of them knows the answer." This is usually a good answer to a fairly routine question of little policy import.

3. **You can respond by saying,**

   "Yes, I know the answer, but it's administrative and so none of your business." This is not a recommended response, though I'm told that until recently it was an acceptable response by some boards from their managers or executives.

*"I don't want any 'yes men' around me.
I want everyone to tell me the truth,
even if it costs them their job."*
—Samuel Goldwyn

RECOGNIZE THE LESSON
OF THE REDWOODS

*"Judgment is not upon all occasions required,
but discretion is."*
—Lord Chesterfield

One way to deal with the issues with which you are con-
fronted is by remembering the redwood trees. You are like the
Redwoods. That is, as you travel about northern California you
see the mighty redwoods standing tall against the sky. Some
of them are 300 feet or even taller. Some have been alive since
Christ was a boy. Almost all of the higher trees are scrawny at
the top, looking like they've been burned at the upper one-
third of their height.

They have been.

Over the period of time that they've been alive, they've
been hit by lightning a number of times. They are kept from
burning and thus destroying the forest by the fact that the redwood bark doesn't burn, it just scorches. But the older the tree
is, the taller it is. And the taller it gets, the more likely it is to
be hit by lightning. Those that are not initially as tall as the
others become the tallest—as the others, over hundreds of

years, are hit by lightning and the lightning blowing off the upper reaches reduces in height the highest trees.

You, too, as you stretch and grow and reach your height, are subjected to being more likely to be hit by lightning, cut down somewhat, your growth slowed for a time, until others outstretch and are themselves hit by lightning.

The challenge, I think, is to keep from thinking you are the lightning—and trying to strike back. But realizing that you are the lightning rod and you will attract the lightning bolt, helps you keep perspective. It's also a reminder to keep your head down somewhat. No matter what your position, you don't have to stick it out all the time. But you do sometime, if you want to stand out. Just know that lightning sometimes strikes.

STRATEGIES FOR CHALLENGE

"Every normal man must be tempted at times,
to spit on his hands,
hoist the black flag,
and begin slitting throats":
—H. L. Mencken

Someday, somebody will go after you. Even the most likable of individuals attracts some animosity. A city hall reporter whom I respected said once about expecting an attack: "A little paranoia heightens awareness." But then she added, "Even paranoiacs have enemies."

Some of the strategies for dealing with enemies or those who don't understand, or, to say it more politically correctly, those who are "comprehendingly challenged" include the

Response Scale, from Do Nothing on the one end to Confrontation on the other.

Response Scale

1	2	3	4	5	6	7	8	9	10
Do Nothing				**Perpetrate a Crisis**					**Confrontation**

On the **Do Nothing** end is to ignore the personal challenge, the affront to your personal strength, the insult to your intelligence or integrity, whatever the challenge is. Just talk about the issues. Smile. And talk about the issues. You are above the personal fray. You cannot be lured into a personality issue.

At the mid-point of the Response Scale is another strategy that some people advocate: To **Perpetrate a Crisis**. Talk about other issues of much greater import. Move on to other items that need urgent attention. Accelerate the action that is needed on big projects.

For example, a Baptist Minister in Texarkana, Arkansas, served the largest Baptist Church in the state. Upon completion of a $5 million building project, he immediately announced the need to begin another $7 million project, "for the education of the youth." When asked privately why he followed one with the other so quickly, he said: "If you don't keep 'em busy on building projects, they'll want to 'talk about the gospel.' And that destroys congregations. And ministers."

When the situation gets ugly and you have done everything you can to avoid the problem, you are at the other end of the scale and that is **Confrontation**. You feel you must deal with the situation up front. You have to say you "can't work with this deal as it is." Then you must offer up the solution in some kind of conflict resolution mode, such as collaboration, that suggests, "Here's how we can work together on that." If that doesn't work and the ugliness continues, you might have to recognize it's not going to get fixed and say, "Maybe I'm the problem, here," and offer to move on.

It's important to recognize that this is a real offer, one that you mean.

This is not a gesture. It's not public relations. It is not an attempt to get the public to come to your support. It is a real offer to be carried out on your shield because the situation is not bearable.

If it is not that kind of a situation, don't use this approach.

We advise staff and children not to ask for something unless they want it, because they just might get it, when we say, "Be careful what you ask for." The same advice is good here. If you use this strategy, it might work that the governing body comes to your aid and fixes the situation. But don't count on it. Have your luggage out when you make this offer.

It is often tempting, when things are stressful and people are being difficult, to offer the devastating riposte. Something like, "For the quality of my lifework, I count on both those people I can call my friends and equally those whom I can call my enemies." Or you might say, "Mr. Brown never passes up an opportunity to prove he's a jerk." It is good to be ready. It is, however, probably the better part of valor to have a weapon at the ready and *not* use it. Quality will out. Stiff upper lip. Show your superiority by your superior behavior.

It is not as much fun, true. You choose your weapon. Ahead of time. Don't wait for the heat of the moment.

Also remember the Book of Job. As one described its

application to innovation or the espousing of new ideas: First they attack the idea; then they attack the person's motivation for initiating the idea; then they attack the integrity of the person initiating the idea. Still, Peter Drucker advises all leaders to "animate by ideas." Even if you do animate some enemies, you've started the ball rolling in the organization and perhaps the community. And as Thoreau said, probably not intending to advocate incremental change, but doing so just the same, "People only believe what they already half-know." So if you espouse an idea, you will animate and some of those animated will be opposed. But while the idea may not be adopted when you propose it, it may cause others to think about it, and in an organizational generation or so, the new idea may become the conventional wisdom.

You won't get the credit, but what the hey, if you wanted the credit, you would have run for President, right?

"In the first two quarters of 2002, U.S. companies engaged in 3,423 layoffs of 50 or more workers, sending more than 693,500 people to unemployment."
—Bureau of Labor Statistics

LAYOFF WARNING SIGNS

What are the chances you will be laid off? Well, the statistics are pretty scary. Management mistakes, management's intentional actions, and faulty business plans can all jeopardize your employment. The economy's volatility can affect even sound operations from time to time. And that's true for private entities, public organizations, and third sector organizations. Knowing it's always easier to get a job while you have a job, the best advice is to keep your eyes and ears open, sensing for the layoff warning signs.

Management Greed

The CEO of Sun Microsystems takes a $30 million salary while Sun stock plummets to single digits. The Tyco CEO takes a $20 million salary while indicted. American Airlines executives solidify their pensions while asking their unions to take a pay cut amounting to $10,000 on each of a $60,000 salary.

When management folks take their money first, they weaken the company. They may say it is a minor amount, but as symbolism for good management, it stinks. Employees need to know that management is looking out for the long term good of the company. Often management takes such an action because they see the trends facing them earlier than others. Enron execs bailed early, knowing the house of cards was about to fall down.

The Finances Are Flawed

If you know something is amiss with the finances of the organization—revenue goals aren't being met, profit goals are not there, there are rumors of mishandled funds, accounts are not being paid, either by the company or to the company, these are all warning signs of flawed finances. If you're in a governmental or nonprofit organization you will know if the economy is down and tax revenues are off or if contributions are off. These are not factors under your control but they can often cause a problem to fall into your lap.

Sharon Watkins of Enron saw something in the numbers that alarmed her. She took what she saw to Ken Lay, figuring he was an honorable man who wanted nothing but good for the company and he would fix it. That was the right approach for her, and while in the short run it got her a new office on a lower floor as a shunning action, in the long run it got her anointed as one of **Time** magazine's Persons of the Year, and on the high dollar speaking circuit. (She was helped by the mistakes and mis-management of several principals at Enron, and whose chickens have not as of this writing totally come home to roost. Chances are they will not fare as well as Ms. Watkins.)

The People Are Changing

The kinds of people being hired are not like the employees there before. It looks like maybe there's a change in strategic thinking that's being reflected by the new folks. Since you're one of the old folks, it might be a precursor that you no longer fit with that thinking. For example, if the accountants used to be green eye-shade basic bean counters and now the new accountants are into creative finance, off-shore shelters, and spinning off assets into new companies with IPO's, there's a definite change in thinking.

Inclusion Becomes Exclusion

You used to be involved in strategic planning decisions, but you've heard they're having a session and you're not invited. That's not a good sign. It works for any other decisions as well. Personnel policy changes, purchasing changes, sales approach changes. Whatever you used to be involved in and you are no longer is a big warning sign that you're no longer a value added commodity to the organization. Find a door to go into before they send you out one.

Ignoring Your Advice

Let's say you have submitted to your boss on your own initiative a new idea, or an idea for improvement or change, and you've not gotten a response. It could be the boss is noodling the idea around and just hasn't gotten back to you. It could be she's having others review it and will respond as soon as they get back to her. And it could be she no longer values your advice, doesn't like the idea, or doesn't care about you needing a response. She may well have you on the short list for layoffs. Any indication the boss isn't listening is a pretty good warning sign.

Bosses Change

Your immediate boss is replaced so you're no longer your boss's hire. Likely the loyalty is not going to be there, certainly not like the loyalty given by the one who hired you. Does he want his own team? Is he making sounds like that? He compares the current troop to his team in his last job, or is often talking about them? It very likely is a warning sign.

The new boss's background is in layoffs. In his last two jobs, he caused major reorganizations, down-sizing, out-sourcing, or other reductions in the size of the work force. That's a pretty good warning sign. How about the top leadership? Have they changed? A whole new regime change is underway? They might be making a short list. You don't have to be in Baghdad to worry about regime change affecting you.

What Do You Do?

So you see these warning signs. One or more. What to do? Consider that John F. Kennedy said, the critical measure "is grace under pressure." You say, "Sure, how do I act with grace under the pressure of losing my job for reasons not within my control?" It's a good question.

Having completed the thought processes in this book will give you a fallback position and will prepare you to handle this pressure. Knowing where you sit financially and knowing who you are and what you value—will help you handle the pressure gracefully. In fact, it may eliminate the pressure.

Everyone needs strong self-esteem. To get a job, to handle a job, to handle job loss. All need strong self-esteem. You have to feel good about yourself to do anything.

C.W. Metcalf, in his book, **_Lighten Up...Survival Skills for People Under Pressure,_** says that the ability to see the "absurdity in adversity (is) a prime component of humor as a survival skill, and (humor is) the key element in remaining creative and healthy under pressure." Find a way to laugh at the potential job loss. What doesn't kill you makes you stronger. The job loss won't kill you. It will make you stronger. Laugh at it. That will build strong self-esteem.

KEEP YOUR FOCUS

> *"Nothing big ever came from being small."*
> **—Donald Trump**

Joann S. Lublin, writing in the Wall Street Journal, suggests that if layoffs loom, you need to stay focused on your career and your job. She suggests there are five coping techniques to help you do that:

1. **"Avoid anger, paralysis, and panic."**
These emotions she points out lead to behaviors that are

destructive and will make it easier for management to toss you off the lifeboat sooner rather than later.

2. **"Concentrate on high-priority tasks that will improve your company's survival chances and bolster your visibility as an adaptive team player."**
   Doing so makes you a more value-added employee and enhances your skills for this job and the next.

3. **"Explore alternative career paths."**
   Create a contingency plan for your dream job, from doing a serious self assessment.

4. **"Intensify your networking efforts."**
   A smart professional, career-long strategy anyway, it works to your advantage now. But as we've said before it's hard to make friends when you need them.

5. **"Maintain a positive attitude."**
   In addition to preparing examples of your best work, for the opportunity to present it to management of this or the next job, do the kinds of things we suggest in the book to get yourself in shape, physically, mentally, and professionally.

Dr. David Morrison does a great deal of work with institutional training in industry and business and government. He says his experience is that the two most stressed professions out there are city managers or executives and general practitioner Medical Doctors. He says the city manager is responsible for everything that happens in his or her city, whether it's the police chief who screws up, a firefighter, or a water line breaks, and the supervising City Council is quick to make him or her a scapegoat. They don't have control over everything personally, they cannot. Too much occurs in a city.

The medical doctors thought they were setting up a practice where they could use their best judgment and treat the whole family as best they could. They find, in contrast, that the medical insurance companies often say a particular test that they want to order on a patient "isn't warranted."

"What do you mean 'isn't warranted'? the doctor asks.

"Ninety percent of the tests come back negative," the insurance rep says, "and it costs a thousand bucks. Since it's 90% unlikely to show anything, it's a waste of money and so is unwarranted."

"That's bogus," says the doctor. "A ten percent rate is considered 'significant' in the scientific community. So you're applying bad science to this decision."

"Well, our experience is nation-wide and it shows that not doing the test makes sense."

The doctor tries to persuade the rep but the rep's got policies that guide his decisions. The judgment of the doctor is not an over-ride of the policy. The doctor is torn between giving the patient what he or she knows in their own mind is the right treatment, but if the insurance won't pay, it will be expensive for the patient, and in fact the hospital or lab may not want to do the test, being at risk at getting their money.

Then the doctor worries about his malpractice insurance. It's costing him or her about the amount the doctor takes home annually, and if he doesn't give a test he feels is warranted and needed, then he's feeling in violation of his oath, and perhaps at risk of malpractice if the patient later develops the condition he's concerned about and dies.

Those pressures are weighing on the doctor and they begin feeling like they're working for the insurance companies, one way or the other. It's not what he signed up to do. He wanted to run his office and serve his patients. He has a nurse, an office assistant, and he's taking orders from lawyers and insurance companies.

So the doctor has an unusual level of stress as well, and things have changed on her, as they've changed for everyone else in society.

Keeping your focus on what's good for you, personally— the results of your exercises showing what you've identified as important for the long haul—help you deal with those changes, including losing your job.

RECOGNIZE THE IMPOSSIBILITY OF THE MANAGEMENT/LEADERSHIP POSITION

No amount of advance planning
can take the place of dumb luck:
—Anon.

Whether you're in public, private, or non-profit, leadership and management are difficult positions with high expectations. Let's look at the similarities, using the example of city management.

A local government manager feels the responsibility for everything. City Councils tend to make them think that way. Individuals will ask them questions in private and be shocked if they don't have an answer. The implication is, "Why did we hire you? We thought we were hiring a professional who knew stuff." The manager should try not to feel guilty. Avoid that inference if it's not spoken. Sure it's tough. The manager is probably the highest paid person in the city government. Council members who ask the questions figure that if they—paid as little as they are—are smart enough to ask the question, the manager—paid as much as she is—should be smart enough and experienced enough to know the answer. The fact is, the executive of city government, is running a large, multi-function corporation, that has a wider range of activity and more individual business units than all but the largest of corporations in the city. Each of the business units has different rules, different goals, and different methods for measuring success.

The private and non-profit sector doesn't have it quite that bad. The City Manager is expected to know everything that goes on in the city, including what the private sector is planning and which grant-funded social service agency is in trouble. The non-public sectors have the same level of expectations only they are confined to the manager's fields of responsibility. Non-profit boards are usually uncompensated and so feel they have the right to ask the tough question even more than if they were paid. Private for-profit boards are often compensated quite handsomely and some are actually selected by the CEO and their compensation set by the Board on the CEO's recommendation. But the pressures to be accountable are growing on the private sector board, and valuable outside directors are being demanded by large institutional investors. These people will ask the hard questions more and more. Shareholders are becoming more active in the private sector, at Annual Meetings, and by virtue of submitting proposals for everything from which companies and countries to do business with, whether to increase dividends, whether to give stock options to employees, and even, employee, officer, and director pay plans. Those meetings are starting to look like council meetings. So far, none of the for-profit mega corporations have televised their Annual Meeting live, though.

For executives, many recruiters say that the profile the councils adopt for the "Ideal City Manager" is illustrative. "Walks on water, but has a sense of humor about it." Or "Has the ability to convert lead into gold, but doesn't take himself (or herself) seriously."

DON'T BE OBSESSED WITH TERMINATION

The late E. Robert Turner, former city manager and private sector executive, said one cannot be a good manager if one is so concerned with security that termination becomes an obsession. He said it's "important that perspective be kept about the need to cause change and the need to survive." He felt he sometimes crossed over from the expected role of the manager, becoming very much a leader, and went too far in suggesting policy approaches that examined local values. From time to time, he said, "I'd have to call and apologize for how demanding I had been," explaining that sometimes he "got the vapors," and lost perspective.

For the non-profit manager, the satisfaction of knowing the good that's being done for the clientele served is its own reward, justifying the risks and hassle. For the private sector there are remunerary rewards beyond the other sectors. A large bonus is a strong salve for past wounds.

MANAGEMENT/LEADERSHIP IS A CAREER TO MAKE A DIFFERENCE IN PEOPLE'S LIVES

Many feel city management is a career that can cause the important change needed in society, and in local government.

It is a "career to make a difference" in the way the world works, in the words of Tom Downs, former Deputy Mayor of Washington, DC. He survived the regime of Mayor Marion Barry, in which the Finance Director was indicted for accepting a $75,000 award from a company to which the city gave a contract, saying, "It was acceptable to that Finance Director to take the money as a 'gratuity for good work'." The Finance Director thought of it as a tip.

Downs made many changes in that city government in his tenure, but he didn't get to change the Finance Director (a Barry appointee) in time.

Many other managers or executives have laid their lives and careers on the line over the years to bring honesty and integrity to city government. They and their families know the sacrifice that they have made. Not that they had to do it at any time or all the time. Just that they chose to do it. The perspective of knowing when to lay it on the line, and for what, is probably the most important perspective for any profession.

We all would like to go out thinking we're being carried out on our shield, as some medieval warrior defending our King, with the public cheering. But the public generally isn't watching.

Or, as noted a couple of generations earlier by Will Rogers, "It's just got so that 90 percent of the people in this country don't give a damn. Politics ain't worryin' this country one tenth as much as parking space." Things haven't changed much. In the 2002 elections, a Washington, D.C. candidate for city council ran on this slogan: "Peace, Justice, Parking." Universal idealism reduced by the knowledge that "All Politics is Local."

Those in the for-profit and non-profit third sector are in careers that make a difference as well. And they wouldn't be continuing on with their careers unless they were. Most people in management positions do not work in a Dilbert cartoon. They do not work with pointy-haired bosses with no clue. They work with co-workers who understand and care about the mission and goals of the organization. Most people like their work. But most people also would like the option of walking away when they felt like it.

Whether we're talking about city managers or executives who are reporting to councils who are elected, and have their own problems, or private managers or executives whose Boards are selected by their compatriots and like-minded associates, the CEO or manager is more and more accountable to its stakeholders for delivery of services and value. They make exciting, significant contributions to society and our world.

Collins and Porras in **Built to Last,** *Successful Habits of Visionary Companies,* pointed out that it didn't matter much what the successful companies were doing, but if they had a clear vision of the goals of the organization and that vision was understood clearly by the employees, that was universally what made those organizations successful. Employees like to know what they're working for, what they're trying to do, and then to feel like they are contributing to that end.

> *"Half of the world is composed of people who have something to say and can't, and the other half who have nothing to say and keep on saying it."*
>
> *—Robert Frost*

HERMAN®

8-13 © 1984 Jim Unger

"Your previous employer says
you're *unpredictable*."

CHAPTER 2

Things I've Always Wanted to Do

"If you can walk, you can dance.
If you can talk, you can sing."
—Zimbabwean Proverb

"As long as you're thinking anyway,
You might as well think big."
—Donald Trump

TAKE A YEAR OF RETIREMENT NOW

You probably began your career thinking you would move from one organization to the next over about 30 years, getting to ever-larger challenges and increasing pay until you retired to your sailboat, if you lived so long. Ask yourself what's wrong with taking that year now. Go to that sailboat. Find a way to afford it. Plan ahead and you face the prospect of separation with some relish.

There are always a lot of things we would like to do. Books we'd like to read. Paths we'd like to walk. Streams we'd like to fish. Art projects to complete.

Make your list of things you would like to do, and that you would do if you didn't have to work. Consider taking a year of retirement now, in mid-career, and do those things. But first, make your list. Make your list with things you'd like to learn, places you'd like to go, recreational things, educational goals, things you'd like to do with your kids. It's not necessary to limit it to 10 items. Many people have made such a list and run it to 300 or more items. Some then begin prioritizing the long list into the list for the next year and the next five years. It becomes a lifetime Goal Plan. Since this list is what you really want to do with the rest of your life, having this list is useful to your psyche. If the things on your list take money, the list might say why you are working after all.

Here's one guy's list of the things he wrote down in the first thirty seconds of the exercise.

THINGS I WANT TO DO:

1. **Write a Novel**

2. **Write a Professional Book**

3. **Build a Solar House**

4. **Learn to Play Piano Well**

5. **Learn to Play Golf Well**

6. **Sail Around the Greek Islands with My Spouse**

7. **Have a Sailboat in San Diego**

8. **Climb Mount Rainier**

9. **Scuba Dive in Cozumel with Sons**

10. **Have My Own Business**

I know many people who keep a lengthy list of lifetime goals and desires of things they want to do and review it often. Then, when the opportunity to do something that's on the list comes along, there's no hesitation in acting. They also know they won't live forever, and expect that at some point they won't be able to do some of these things, so they had better get to it.

It's been said that half of all the people who have ever lived on earth are alive today. So then statistically, each of us has a one in two chance of ever dying. But do you want to believe the statistical evidence in this case or do you want to believe your eyes? So, you'd better make that list and then get to it.

Once you've made your list, ask yourself this question: "What would I do if given two years to live?" That prioritizes your list. Take that list of items and put them at the top. Then ask "What would I do if given one year to live?" That makes a smaller list and the more important items are at the top. Then ask, "What would I do if given six months to live?" That's an even shorter list and it's absolutely your most important, highest priority goals. And it makes you want to get to those, doesn't it?

No matter how long you live, it's been said, you're going to leave this earth with a full in-basket. Things undone. But if you make yourself a set of lists like this, those things left to do will not be the most important things to you. You will have done the most important.

The exercise puts in perspective your life, your values, your life goals. Makes the termination or layoff much less a problem for you. Perspective does that.

PLAY

You may have always wanted to play the piano, but never seemed to have the time, or you were distracted by the pressures of your job. Think of losing your job and focusing your efforts three or four hours a day on learning how to play the piano well. You could do it. What a great sense of accomplishment that would be. Particularly at your advanced age. The mental health benefits would be exceptional. The part of the brain that is fed by piano lessons is not the same part as that used in management work. I don't know if that's right brain/left brain creativity versus logic or if it's a much more sophisticated subdivision of the brain. But I'm confident that the effort to learn the piano, while difficult, would be mentally refreshing; it's like resting a section of the brain that had been running on high for a long while.

All of us would like to play golf or tennis well. The same benefits hold as with the piano. But there are also the physical benefits. Physical exercise is a great stress reducer as is the mental change to piano lessons. So you can play, learn new skills, and build greater health at the same time.

It sounds so good, you might just quit working right now! "Fallback Position? Hell, that's my life plan."

MAKE MONEY WITH YOUR HOBBY

"The best revenge is living well":
—George Herbert

Do What You Love and The Money Will Follow is a book and a phrase that is popular today. It speaks to the fact that you can do what you want and live well, too. It can happen; you just have to have faith and confidence that it will.

LIVE OFF YOUR WITS: THAT'S WHAT YOU'VE BEEN DOING ANYWAY

"Our doubts are traitors,
And make us lose the good we oft might win
On fearing to attempt."
—Lucio, Measure for Measure

Look at all the changes that are occurring out there. Certainly, you can find something that you like doing, if only for a short time, that fits the needs of society. Call it recharge-the-batteries time. Call it a respite. But find something to do with your knowledge: consult, teach, start a business, write, or invent something.

Remember Thomas Edison. The conventional wisdom regards him as a pure researcher, sitting in a lab and tinkering until something was developed like the electric light bulb. But that's not how he worked. He had one of the first research and development labs. He instructed his people to think of what people needed, and then try to find a way to provide it. In that sense, he was more of a market analysis innovator than an inventor. But the inventor role is more the stuff of legend. Still he invented dozens of products.

Maybe you can find a way to provide something that society needs. Somebody had to develop the safety pin, Velcro, suitcases on wheels, and everything else you can think of. Hop to it.

PUT YOUR SKILLS TO WORK

There are many opportunities out there for "Interim Work." Can you be a supervisor, an advisor, a coach? A little like consulting, a short-term interim position can be a lot of fun. It can be a bit of a respite. It's a great way to make new contacts, help support a new staff, and make new friends. Since my contacts tend to be in city governance, I've known several managers or executives who have done interim work and prefer it. Al Locke left the city of Kirkland, Washington, after serving 20 years as city manager. Since then he has served as interim manager for many local governments. He has found it an enjoyable way to provide service and keep his hand in. "I don't work summers," he declares. This type of thing is equally true of men and women in the private sector. With down-sized companies, the opportunities abound.

Many private consulting firms provide interim services around the country. Temporary service and manpower agencies have exploded around the world. The Internet provides a host of resources that search engines will find.

Interim management and executive temping have become more popular and are considered legitimate ways to continue using knowledge gained in a career.

It happens in government, as well in the non-profit sector, and was invented in the for-profit sector, as part of the outsourcing approach. Whether your background is public or private, non-profit or for-profit, there are interim positions to be had. Retired volunteers are often used by non-profits to fill vacant executive positions. The Senior Corps is a good example of the concept being institutionalized. Getting qualified people to fill positions that can't go a long time vacant is a critical issue in most organizations. You can try out many of them while you look for a permanent position. But you might get to be like Al Locke and choose interim positions for the rest of your career. The future of interim management is strong.

WHAT DO YOU WANT FOR YOURSELF?

It's important to integrate your goals with your values in any life planning or "futures exercise", in order to be meaningful for the long-term. A good way to do that is used in private business. Called "Woody-Woofy," for the WDYWFY near-acronym, the concept is all about What Do You Want For Yourself. It's what motivates you to keep going day after day. It's mental sustainability in the working environment.

One friend of mine, whose name will remain anonymous for reasons that will become obvious, followed this approach and wrote down what is important to him to keep him going. He keeps it in his Franklin Planner and refers to it daily, when he's in boring meetings, or waiting on someone who's not being very hospitable. Here's what his list is:

"THE PLACE I WANT TO WORK:

- *Environment with informal hierarchical structure*
- *Environment where both team-work and individually-based work is valued*

- *Fun, humor-filled*

- *Fast-paced, dynamic*

- *Uses cutting-edge technology*

- *Promotes a balance between personal life and work*

- *Recognizes accomplishments and quality work, especially through compensation and benefits structures*

- *Leadership with the vision to move the organization forward and the confidence to let it happen*

- *Trust*

- *Straightforward, low-key resolution of conflict*

- *Autonomy to achieve mission/goals with the support of leadership managing product, not process*

- *Ability to be creative, innovative, and continuously learning, developing new skills*

- *Variety in assignments, relatively few rote tasks*

- *Some travel, but not substantial*

- *Few evening and weekend commitments*

- *Enterprising, seeks new ways to add value to our customers*

- *Opportunities to develop mentoring or mutually-growth-oriented relationship with my boss*

- *Public service orientation*

- *Inspire others around me*

- *High expectations of me and those above and below"*

This listing is a good example of a thoughtful approach to what's important to you in the working environment. Different from the life planning lists, in that they look beyond the job,

WDYWFY looks specifically at what psychic rewards you want to get out of the job. Beyond money. The exercise requires you to ponder and really think about what's important in the working environment to keep you mentally alive and to keep the creative juices flowing. Many working environments are not supportive, are even stifling, and as you prepare your fallback position, what you need and want is important to know. If you're not working within your WDYWFY environment, in large part, then you're likely to be in trouble at some point.

WHAT YOU DON'T WANT

> *"Lord, please let me die peacefully in my sleep,*
> *like my grandfather,*
> *and not like his screaming passengers."*
> **—Internet prayer**

There are things in life that we know we don't want. There are people we know we don't want to work with. There are bosses we know we don't want to work for. There are jobs we know we don't want to work at.

In other words, it's very clear and we're very certain as to what it is we **don't want**. That's a list we also need to make. It, too, is a life-clarifying list, a value clarification list that helps us plan our future.

Make yourself a list of those things you know you don't want. (This is not like the high school senior who, when ask what they want to do in life, say, "I just want to be happy." That's the unexamined prescription for happiness that will never be achieved. I suspect it's most often expressed by an adolescent that sees parents arguing and figures they're not happy, not understanding that some conflict is natural and the ability to work it out with each other in a marriage is a form of happiness.)

You make your own list, but some of the things that I've heard people say they don't want are provided here to give you a leg up in thinking about what you don't want:

- *A job with no room for growth.*
- *A boring job, routine tasks done over and over.*
- *A boss who is inconsistent or can't make a decision.*
- *A boss who is unreasonable.*
- *A boss who doesn't treat people right.*
- *A boss who doesn't respect my need to decide when I can go on vacation.*
- *A boss that doesn't trust me to know when I'm too sick to work.*

You make your own list. Don't use this one. The point is, it's just as important to know what we don't want as it is to know what we want.

GOAL SPECIFIC DIRECTION

"Dr. Phil", Phillip C. McGraw in his book, **Strategies,** talks about the *Seven Step Strategy* for acquiring your goals.

1. **"Express your goal in terms of specific events or behaviors.**

2. **"Express your goal in terms that can be measured.**

3. **"Assign a timeline to your goal.**

4. **"Choose a goal you can control.**

5. **"Plan and program a strategy that can get you to your goal.**

6. **"Define your goal in terms of steps.**

7. **"Create accountability for your progress toward your goal."**

This seven-step strategy is not unlike the other exercises in this book about knowing what you want and organizing to get it. His seven steps are included here to expand and reinforce the approach you need to find a fallback position.

HERMAN®

1-10 © 1976 Jim Unger

"Have a good vacation. I've decided not to
give you your bad news until you get back."

CHAPTER 3

Things To Do Right Away If You're Fired: Financial

Many experts in financial planning say there are specific things you should immediately do if you are laid off. These actions are necessary for you to prepare in advance for that happening as well.

Recognize that panic is one of the first emotions you'll feel. You're used to looking down the road and preparing for the unknown. You look around and you see the unemployment rate is high, people are talking on the air waves about how hard it is to get a job in today's market, and you immediately go to the worst case scenario: What if I never get another job? The homeless often say you're just a few months away from being out here with me. A bad health experience can put you out of your house. You start to breathe hard, your heartbeat goes up. You can visualize all kinds of disasters for you, your family, your kids.

So get a grip on that emotion, and sit down and rationally figure out where you are. Don't let fear paralyze you.

You have a budget now, and you figure out how much money you have and how long it will last on that budget. Most recruiters say it takes one month per each $10,000 of salary you seek. So figure if you have enough money to last that long. Susan Abentrod of the outplacement firm, Transition Team, says, "…older people or those in bad job markets may find that their search goes on much longer."

Many financial planners offer advice for how to stretch your money for the necessary number of months. Here's what most all agree and say:

- *Use your severance money to pay expenses,* not as a windfall for debt reduction.

- *Understand your organization's COBRA costs.* Health insurance is one of the most expensive items in your social safety net. Most people don't realize how much it costs, when the organization was paying a healthy share for the employee. Under COBRA the laid off employee has 18 months of mandatory coverage if the organization has over 20 employees. And in some cases that can be extended another 12 months. But the former employee pays the full cost, plus a little for administration. Look around for another, lower cost plan but don't let the COBRA lapse until you have it.

- *Create a layoff budget,* which is just basic living expenses and minimum payments. See how long that makes your money stretch. Abentrod suggests if your minimum budget is down to four months, consider calling your creditors for payment moratoriums. The Consumer Credit Counseling Service can assist. 800-388-2227.

- *Don't use credit cards.*

- If you lost life insurance from the organization through the layoff, **keep protecting your family with the lowest cost term insurance you can find.**

- *Consider applying for unemployment.* Recognize that every payment extends the time your money will last. Check out in advance what that payment will be in your state. Go to www.findlaw.com and you can chase down your state's payments.

- ***Roll you lump-sum distributions from a 401 (k) or other retirement plan into another IRA.*** *Amy White of Clayton Financial Services, Inc. says that "If the company is laying people off and has therefore indicated it is troubled, why would you want to leave your retirement money there for them to manage? Get control of it right away, and put it to work for you. You don't want to use that money for living expenses, since it will be taxed and have penalties if you do. So roll it into another IRA and forget about it." A caveat she offers is, "Use that money only to prevent becoming homeless!"*

TERMINATION AGREEMENTS NEED CARE

"He who frames the argument often wins it":
—George Will

WHAT YOU NEED TO KNOW ABOUT TERMINATION AGREEMENTS

At the time of a separation, you are in no mood to be rational. You have severed the relationship, and you would like to move on and get to another stage in your life. So your interest in the termination agreement is not great. But your attention needs to be focused on the future and the options that you may have if you protect them, and that you may lose if you don't. Since, in your mind, the termination agreement is dealing with the past, you don't have the focus on the future that you need. These exercises help you to know in advance what you need to think about and why.

We all expect that once a relationship is severed, we will walk across the street the next day and be scooped up by some other employer. After all, we've been a successful value-added employee and we know some important stuff.

The truth is that sometimes happens, but it usually does not. On average it takes about six months to land another job. And paradoxically, the higher you are in your profession— money, size of organization—the harder it is to find a job. You need to protect against the catastrophic occurrence of an extended period of unemployment.

This assumes, of course, that you are not independently wealthy, that your spouse cannot support you in the style to which you've become accustomed, and that the other circum- stances of your life are not such that you don't need an income. If this assumption doesn't apply to you, you don't need this book, but you probably didn't read this far anyway. For the rest of us, preparation for catastrophe is just a sensible precaution.

Many people assume a termination clause in the employ- ment agreement is like a pre-nuptial agreement—in which trust in a loving relationship is integral. But you are not marrying the organization or the governing body, though the similarities are often cited. If you are preparing yourself for the future well and preparing your organization well, there will be some definition in the employment agreement of how termination occurs. Then when you get to the point of completing a termination agree- ment, you will find the process much easier.

Appendix C provides a sample termination agreement. All of its provisions may not apply to you and your situation, but it offers some useful paragraphs for your consideration. And a good deal of that needs to be in the Employment Agreement.

PHRASEOLOGY CAN AFFECT BENEFITS

*"The most valuable of all talents is that of
never using two words when one will do."*
—Thomas Jefferson

———

Just the way the Termination Agreement is phrased can make a big difference in the benefits you may be entitled to. Subtleties in the law and bureaucratic interpretations will call for all the advance planning and attention you can give them.

TAX BENEFIT AS CASUALTY LOSS

The agreement can be phrased in such a way that a certain amount of any severance paid can be tax-deductible. If you get a lump sum severance that bumps your total tax liability up, such a phrase can be a savings to you of considerable proportions. And you may need it the next year. Court rulings have addressed the phrasing in the Termination Agreement that will make this tax benefit possible. In the section under Useful Phrases, one suggestion that has been adjudged qualified is provided. Your attorney and tax consultant of course will be the best advisors on the subject.

One tax-adviser writes as follows:

"Damages for defamation tax free"
Damages received in a lawsuit for personal injuries are tax free. In lawsuits involving defamation claims, the IRS holds that damages are tax free only if they are compensation for injury to personal reputation. Damages allocable to business

reputation are taxed as a replacement of lost earnings.

The Tax Court, with appeals court support, rejected the IRS distinction and held that if defamation is a personal injury under state law, all of the damages are tax free even if the injury has business consequences (Threlkeld, 87 T.C. 1294 (1986).

The IRS has continued to litigate the issue. It recently asked the Tax Court to reconsider its Threlkeld position and to adopt the IRS distinction between injury to personal reputation and injury to business reputation. The Tax Court not only reaffirmed its position, but held that tax-free treatment applies to punitive damages as well as compensatory damages for personal injuries.

Miller sued her employer and two of its officers after being falsely accused of embezzlement. In a settlement, she received $900,000, which was reduced to $525,000 after deducting legal fees and other costs.

The IRS claimed that the entire settlement was taxable as compensation for damage to business reputation. Further, even if the compensatory damages are tax free, punitive damages do not qualify for the exclusion from income.

The Tax Court held the entire settlement was tax free. The statute (Code Section 104) provides tax-free treatment for all damages on account of personal injuries; this includes punitive damages. Since under state law (Maryland) defamation is an action for personal injury, the exclusion applies.

Dissenting judges argued that the punitive damages

should not be treated as an award for personal injuries. Under Maryland law, punitive damages do not compensate an injured party for harm suffered, but are intended to punish the wrongdoer in an attempt to deter similar conduct.

—Your Income Tax, p. 12-14
Miller, 93 TC No 29"

UNEMPLOYMENT ELIGIBILITY DETERMINED

Here again, the phrases in the Termination Agreement can determine whether you are immediately eligible for unemployment compensation or not. In most all states, you are eligible for unemployment compensation if you have been fired or laid off. This may be so even if your exit is labeled as "early retirement." Now you may not want unemployment, feeling you are above it, not want it on your record that you took unemployment, or that you would just be embarrassed. But we're looking further down the road here, when you are in a catastrophic situation and the jobs just aren't coming your way, your daughter is ready to go to college, and the bills aren't getting paid on time.

In some states, who collects unemployment is considered privileged, private information, and so is nobody's business. This might be true in yours. The fact would be worth knowing in advance if you are sensitive to that issue. In any case, we advise practicality take precedence over pride.

WORKERS COMPENSATION

In some places in this country, Workers Compensation is so liberally interpreted that "stress" is considered cause for a WC claim. In California at one point, only 10% of the cause of stress had to be from the job. What manager of people could not claim stress to the level of 10% from the job? That provision has since been changed so that 51% of the stress has to be job-related in order to have a valid claim.

No one wants to be involved in fraud, however. Avoiding making a claim that isn't truly justified would fit most people's value systems.

DON'T RUSH TO THE AGREEMENT WITHOUT ASSISTANCE

"I just want to end it":
—Resigning manager

Most executives are accustomed to writing agreements and contracts and so rightly feel competent in doing so on their own termination. But that's like defending yourself in a court case. And we all remember the Lincoln admonition about that: "A lawyer who represents himself has a fool for a client."

When you are in the turmoil of a termination, even the most pleasant, the potential for ill will and acrimony is there. If you've been through it all, or close to someone who has been through it, you know there is blame yet to come, there is innuendo, rumor, and uninformed commentary that will be hurtful, all yet to come.

Like the friends you knew who were getting a divorce and said it would be the "friendliest divorce ever." You said, "Right" to yourself with considerable doubt, and you were correct. They ended up acrimoniously fighting over every last piece of chattel. Termination takes big people acting above themselves to handle it well without it eventually becoming a dogfight.

An attorney with experience in the field will be a help to you in these times. Chances are you know some attorney with experience as special counsel on personnel-related issues, with little likelihood of a conflict of interest with your organization or the people in it.

GET A SURROGATE TO NEGOTIATE FOR YOU

*"Everything has been said
but not everyone has yet said it."*
—Senator Bob Dole

One manager friend of mine after seven years in a city was pressured for months to resign. He kept trying to land another job but the cities offering jobs were not professionally or personally attractive to him. After seven months, he was tired of the snide comments made to him by his Mayor and other council members and was ready to resign. He was simply going to use his accrued vacation as a month's severance, resign, and walk away from it all.

I gave him some suggestions and things to think about, but he indicated he was just fed up with the situation and wanted to end the pressure and be done talking to them.

He told me that, and I advised him to get a lawyer to call the Mayor and suggest that the manager would like to resign and make the separation non-controversial and pleasant for all; that to do so he would need salary and benefits paid for some months; further the attorney could make it clear (without threatening) that otherwise the Mayor and Council could vote to fire him in public and it would become an issue for the elected officials. After all, I told him, the council had been pressuring him privately and so had likely violated the open meetings law—by sharing information on how they would vote and then communicating that without benefit of a noticed meeting. The attorney could use that if it came to a hardball negotiation, while he personally would not be comfortable doing so.

But most people are reluctant to get an attorney, thinking it will permanently disfigure their smiling face of a reputation. Although while Shakespeare's Claudio in **Much Ado About Nothing** advises against advice by saying, *"Let every eye negotiate for itself, And trust no agent,"* there are times when it is necessary and proper to have an agent negotiate for you. One of those times is when you and the other party to the negotiation are emotionally involved in the decision and that emotion interferes with negotiation. Clearly if you've been fired or laid off, you're emotionally involved, and likely the supervisor who made the decision is as well. After all, they don't want their judgment on the decision questioned and you don't agree with the decision.

THE LABOR LAWYER IS USEFUL

Many executives and managers would find it distasteful to hire a labor lawyer to represent them. They have had too many bad experiences on the other side of the table. They might even think the labor lawyer is without principle or integrity. But the techniques of hardball negotiation as applied to your final severance and security in a tough situation may be just what the doctor ordered to make you well.

The labor lawyer also can argue the points you would not like to or could not debate well. He or she can articulate the problems of finding another job and the need to protect the family. All the tear-jerking arguments you've heard the labor lawyer play on you, and perhaps your governing body or employer, can be used to your benefit.

CURRENT LEGAL ISSUES AND HUMAN RESOURCE TRENDS

The law regarding employment and termination is a living, growing, evolving animal. Any book will be out of date as soon as the next court meets with a case on the subject. But it's important to talk at least a little bit about the state of the law regarding termination, so you can look at the issues.

Joann S. Lublin of the **Wall Street Journal** reports that even big bosses getting fired often sue for huge amounts for wrongful termination. That leads to prolonged and costly legal battles and companies are trying to find ways to avoid such lawsuits. Alternative dispute resolution devices are being put in place, including mediation and arbitration, and companies are making such apply to "nearly every non-union employee from the highest officer on down." The higher officers need to be included because the stakes are higher. The executive gets the company's attention when they sue for tens of millions of dollars.

Wrongful discharge suits can drag on for three to six years, she reported. That gives great opportunity for the employee to settle for a lesser amount and save on attorney's fees.

For the employee preparing a fallback position, knowing the trends in employment law is important. The single most important trend, Peter Drucker reports in **Managing for the Future,** is that the job is becoming more and more a "property right" of the employee, leading to the need for due process to be exercised. If it's not, there is a flaw that can be exploited by the terminated employee. And even a mediocre lawyer can usually find a flaw in the due process used by an employer. Usually it's the "genesis flaw:" the employer didn't begin informing the employee of performance problems soon enough, so the employee didn't have a chance to correct the problems before the employer was prejudiced against the employee.

Progressive discipline was not used soon enough, it can be argued, or it began before the employee was aware there was even a hint of a problem.

Employees are usually terminated, Drucker reports, "because of three factors: (1) attendance problems, (2) conduct or not following work rules, including insubordination, or (3) performance problems, including not completing tasks according to policies and procedures. Of the three, performance is the hardest to use and offers the most risk of being overturned or producing a judgment in favor of the terminated employee in a wrongful discharge suit."

Another key trend in employment is the concept of ***discipline without punishment.*** That has the advantage of putting the employee in charge of correcting the behavior rather than having the supervisor make sure the employee's behavior changes through using progressive discipline leading up to discharge.

Defamation suits are also out there and growing. Firing an employee for a transgression and then making an example of them for the other employees is a big no-no in today's litigious environment. This is particularly true if the employee was fired for something that could be considered criminal, such as stealing, but was never convicted. The employer who makes an example is likely to be granting a large award to the employee when the jury finally comes in.

Mary E. Reid writing the *Manager's Journal* column of the **Wall Street Journal** asks "What is a defamatory statement?" and then answers it, as "...any statement deemed capable of damaging a person's reputation. Common examples...include:

- *A statement criticizing an employee's job performance, specifically if it implies incompetence or inability to perform.*

- *A statement accusing an employee of a crime.*

- *A statement implying insubordination or disruption of workplace harmony.*

- *A statement involving lack of integrity in the performance of employment duties (e.g. alcoholism, lack of ethics, dishonesty or untrustworthiness)."*

Courts have been rewarding whistle-blowers who are fired as a "retaliatory act." If the employee who has a good record and little or no documentation against them, blows the whistle on some wrong-doing and then is fired, that employee has a good shot at suing and receiving a sizeable award. Sometimes the employee just wants the job back, and those suits are often successful as well. Employers need to be aware of those trends, but it's also useful for the employee preparing a Fallback Position.

I have brimming files of news articles of whistle-blowers getting large awards. L.A. Transit paid $1.2 million for terminating two former investigators for "exposing fraud," the AP reported. They settled on the courthouse steps just before the trial, as is common.

A Sonoma County hospital employee won her job back, after the County had spent $110,000 fighting her dismissal. She charged it was because she revealed fraud and corruption in her hospital double billing patients or their insurance companies. She said the radiology department would require additional x-rays, CAT scans, or procedures that weren't necessary, but duplicated the diagnosis activity. And it was routine, she said.

After re-instatement, she pursued a civil suit for damages. This is a good example of the public interest argument playing out over a whistle-blower, and as far as health care goes, it seems we need more watchful employees and whistle-blowers. We could use it with utility billing and credit card billing as well.

Time magazine elevated private and public sector whistle-blowing in 2002 by making Persons of the Year each of the three women employees of WorldCom, Enron, and the FBI.

BREACH OF CONTRACT SUITS

Another course of action being followed by some, usually the higher-end executive who gets fired, is to file a lawsuit asserting breach of contract. Time-Warner, Inc fired the head of Warner Music U.S. "for cause," they said. He filed a $50 million lawsuit for breach of contract, the *Wall Street Journal* reported. That's happened so often that now many companies are adopting alternative dispute resolution mechanisms, including binding arbitration after a panel of peers or others review the facts of the situation and give the employee a hearing. As Peter Drucker says, the property right to the job argument is a rising trend.

FEDERAL LAYOFF LAW

A surprising twist to the federal layoff law is that investment bankers and stock traders have been suing former employers for failing to give them 60 days notice, as required by the law. All employers need to be aware of the WARN Act, the Worker Adjustment and Retraining Notification Act, "designed by Congress to compensate blue-collar workers when plants are closed," reports Michael Siconolfi writing in the **Wall Street Journal.**

Siconolfi quoted attorney David Wechsler, "It doesn't matter whether the worker is at a Wall Street firm or an auto plant, …you have to give them the proper notice—or a bare minimum of wage payout" as compensation.

SEVERANCE PAY

No law requires that a fired or laid off employee be given severance pay. But most companies and organizations do. The usual rule of thumb for severance pay for workers is one week pay for each year on the job. Some organizations make that two weeks pay. It's still not very much, and it varies by occupation and industry. Here's an example of the percentage of industries paying severance for officers and executives, for the number of years served.

Severance for Managers or Executives and Professionals by Years of Service

When severance is calculated based on years of service only.

70 to 90% of all industries give one to two weeks per year of service. That's clearly the most common calculation.

Many human resource firms and specialists counsel, as this

PERCENTAGE RECEIVING				
Severance pay per year of service*	Officers	Senior executives	Executives	Managers or executives and salaried professionals
Less than one week	5%	4%	4%	6%
One week	43	44	47	60
Two weeks	28	28	32	30
Three weeks	5	5	5	3
One month	12	13	11	5
More than one month	14	11	7	2

book does, to include severance in the termination provisions of your initial contract. If you don't have a formal agreement, you will likely have a letter that provides the terms and conditions of your employment and it should include the termination provisions and how much severance is provided, in case of termination or layoff, but also in case of merger or acquisition that makes your job superfluous. If you don't get that initially, and you had the discussion with the hiring authority, send your own letter to the hiring authority, saying you understand that upon one of the events causing the loss of job, except perhaps for cause, you will get the following severance provisions. That then may become an implied contract if there is a later dispute.

While it is tempting to just rush into the new marriage with no thought of it ever ending, it is the better part of valor and love to use as much discretion as is practical on the way in. After all, these folks are your friends at this time. When they're under the crunch later to trim staff and cut costs to save their own jobs, perhaps, they won't be. Make the deal with your friends.

THE TAX ACCOUNTANT IS IMPORTANT

*"The hardest thing in the world to understand
is the income tax":*
—Albert Einstein.

Nobody knows your finances and the tax law like your accountant. It's worth his fee to spend an hour with him or her and review the elements of your situation that need action before and after your termination. Tax law is ever-changing and most of us cannot keep up on every obscure provision, particularly the court cases that have set precedent. Moreover, most managers or executives do not keep up on those provisions that may only apply in the case of a termination.

CREATE A MOTIVATION TO AGREE

*"Nine-tenths of the serious controversies
which occur in life
result from misunderstanding."*
—Louis D. Brandeis

You would think there would be a mutual motivation to agree to a separation agreement, by whatever terminology it's called. Both the executive and the governing body want to sever the relationship amicably and handle the organization's business well. So it ought to be easy to work out a separation that presents the best face to the public, right? Uh-uh. Often, unfortunately, that motivation gets sublimated to the perceived need to extract a pound of flesh.

As many have pointed out, there are three phases to a group:

Getting to Know You:	*The Introductory Phase*
Working Together Effectively:	*The Efficiency Phase*
Separation:	*The End Phase*

Each needs to be handled just as well as the other for humans to be humane and professionals to be professional. It helps for the morale of those staying behind and those coming into the organization if the last separation was handled humanely.

Whenever a new hire is brought onto staff, people work hard to make the newby feel welcome, introducing them around, taking them into the groups that go to lunch, and building a team spirit. If there's a board relationship, there are social events, professional events, and the newby is included. The introductory phase is the honeymoon and it's a lot of fun. Everyone has high hopes it will continue forever.

Then there is the working together phase. During it there will be disagreements. The most human, sensitive, caring, mature, and growing individuals will make this period the most productive and goal-achieving. It will be a time of making important changes and accomplishment that all can be proud of. Sometimes the direction is not unanimous, the employee is not supported in the direction by all members of the board, or the hiring authority thinks actions haven't been handled quite right, and the relationship gets out of sync. Then it's time for a retreat, a 'time out' to regroup, re-coordinate, and get back together on direction. Often the relationship gets back on track. But sometimes it doesn't. The hiring authority has changed or changed direction and the manager or employee doesn't fit the new direction.

Then the employee is at the End Phase, which ought to be handled with as much humanity as the Introductory Phase. But often it is not.

As an object lesson of how bad it can get, I know of one city manager who was fired by his governing body; the Mayor asked a police sergeant to accompany him to his office where he was given fifteen minutes to clear out his belongings, and then he was escorted from the building. Since there were no charges of impropriety involved, it was purely an inhumane and demeaning act, probably retributive and ego-building on the Mayor's part.

Sometimes that happens in the private sector today, under the guise of fearing sabotage of the computer system. People are told they are laid off at the very same time as their computer is being disabled. They are given a limited amount of time to clean out the office and leave. Security is provided to protect management from office violence.

AVOID WORKPLACE VIOLENCE

There is no need for that kind of inhumane treatment. There is enough stress in being told you're not needed any longer, the organization doesn't need to pile it on—particularly at the time when the discharged employee is feeling he or she gave the organization so much and then has just been jettisoned.

Fortune magazine, in an article on workplace violence, noted that before 1980 there were no reports of violence in the workplace. However, since 1980, there have been an average of 18 shootings a year in the workplace that killed more than one person. Many were multiple murders, with a suicide following. Multiples more didn't result in death. That speaks to the need for humane treatment of employees through *all* phases of the relationship.

Of the top six warning signs for workplace violence, the feeling of having been wronged by the organization or its executive is at the top. The most often cited reason employees feel mistreated is how they were notified of the termination. Research shows that the way to terminate an employee follows these guidelines:

1. The Employer Needs to Provide Fair and Sensitive Treatment

- *The Employer Needs to Be Honest and Straightforward with the Employee*

- *The Employer Needs to Give the Employee Advance Notice of the Termination*

- *The Employer Needs to Treat the Employee with Dignity and Respect*

- *The Employer Needs to Reduce the Financial Burden on the Employee's Family by Providing Severance and Benefits*

- *The Employer Needs to Allow the Employee to Comment on the Termination*

- *The Employer Needs to Offer Counseling for Psyche Shock: "Little Death"*

- *The Employer Needs to Offer Outplacement Services*

2. The Termination Meeting: The Most Important

Part of the Process

The treatment an employee receives at the termination meeting often determines whether the employee feels wronged and will sue or take another action.

How the Employer Breaks the News and Gives Reasons Leads to:

- *Whether the Employee Sues*

- *Whether the Employee Works the Other Employees Against the Employer*

- *Whether the Employee Sabotages the Organization on the Way Out*

- *Whether the Employee Resorts to Violence*

3. The Termination Meeting: *Who, Where, How, and When*

The employee expects to be treated well even in termination. We all believe we have a right to expect that from our employer. Knowing how to terminate employees humanely is something every employee and every manager can bring to the job and add value to their employment. That's an addition to the fallback position of another kind. So as you prepare your fallback position and move through the value exercises, finding critical human resources skill sets that you bring to the organization and your boss or employer can help you be the last tossed off the lifeboat.

Who: **Just the Immediate Supervisor and the Employee
—Unless the Employer Feels the Need for an
HR Person**

Where: **The Employee's Office:
—Allows the Employee to Come Out On
Their Own**

When: **Friday Afternoon
—Allows the Employee to Clean Out the Desk on
the Weekend**

I would advise anyone fired and escorted from the office by police to realize they are being treated badly, and to insist the police put cuffs on them, and then make certain someone sees him being escorted out. Why? Because that's pretty much prima facie evidence of mistreatment and defamation. It's hard to think of those things when you're being humiliated, however. But it can be part of your plan.

A better plan is to have an Employment Agreement that includes a Termination Provision, which includes how the termination will be handled, and which also includes a statement for the staff and public. Most of us don't want to fuss with that when we're coming in because we think all will be well. But things change and stuff happens. A fallback position is having that put in place up front. Doing so is good business. You can show the hiring authority that you're value-added for the organization because you're showing the company an easy way out if things don't work. In effect, you're offering the company a fallback position if your hiring turns out not to fit. The Sample Employment Agreement in Appendix B provides a couple of examples. But don't rely on those alone. Get your attorney involved.

THE BOSS YOU SIGNED ON WITH MAY NOT BE THERE LONG

"Who are those guys?":

—Butch Cassidy

One of the reasons people need to consider the fallback position is because things change. Among the factors that change are the members of the governing body, the management, or the hiring authority. In today's volatile, ever-changing work environment, the folks who hired you and initially loved you often will be replaced. Sometimes the replacements will think less of you than the originals, will think of you as a supporter of the originals—whom they may have just defeated in an acrimonious fight—or otherwise just replaced. And they may feel they need to make a change in direction. You may be considered to be looking backward rather than forward at the new direction. You may be thought of as dragging your feet.

One specialized group illustrates.

The public city manager is probably most in need of a fallback position—more so than the private sector or the non-profit. There aren't many positions today in which you sign onto a job from which the bosses can discharge you at will, and the bosses themselves can be replaced regularly. That's an unusual amount of ambiguity, even in today's constantly changing world.

Being a city manager is a lot like being a lion trainer: sometimes they do what you want but there's usually a lot of growling and fang-bearing, and every once in a while you get bit in the butt.

Being a manager of any enterprise is also much like taking your dog for a walk. In this analogy, the manager is the Dog, and the hiring authority is the Walker.

The Walker lets the Dog go way out in front and on down the path, just as long as the Dog keeps looking back to see if she's going in the right direction. Then occasionally the Walker changes direction, and the Dog has to run like hell to catch up and get out in front again. And the Walker sometimes changes direction just so the Dog will have to change too.

When I first became a city manager 30 years ago, the average term of office was 5 1/2 years. It's now about 3 1/2. Some dogs can't catch up to the constant changes in the route of the walk. Some quit trying.

But whether you're in public or private sector, you have some hiring authority that you need to keep up with, stay out in front of, and assess continuously whether you're still going in the same direction. It's particularly true for new employees, when the employee should be going somewhat slowly, trying to figure out the culture and norms in the new organization, but is trying to show ability to perform by moving fast. The new employee has to be careful not to get out of sync with the organization or the bosses, particularly the boss that hired them. The boss's reputation is on the line as well.

One employee in my experience was the poster child for how not to enter a new organization. She was the director of finance, a Chief Financial Officer, in charge of a number of operations, including purchasing and contracts. She went into the purchasing office her first week and told the assembled staff, "I know more than you do, so just do things the way I tell you and we'll get along fine." She doubled her bad bet by going to the Human Resources Office and yelling at staff there for not doing what she wanted done. That office wasn't even one of her reports. She lasted less than a year, partly because the boss who hired her had an investment in her and ignored her transgressions. She was never effective and became the butt of several jokes—the object lesson of bad supervisory behavior—while she was there and after she left. As Carol Hymowitz has reported in Marketplace, her "In The Lead" column, "Never ignore your company's culture and power structure. No matter how savvy your strategy, it will fail without the bosses' support."

WRONGFUL TERMINATION

"You Cain't Do That":
—*Elvis Presley in* Love Me Tender

—∞∞—

Wrongful termination in the public sector is often used by employees below the level of Department Head. Rarely is it applicable to the Department Head or public executive. In the private sector, it's happening more and more at the employee level and occasionally at the executive level. When a Wall Street Investment Banking executive was fired, he sued for wrongful termination and sought $40 million. That's a negotiation strategy, recognizing that proper risk management suggests settling for a fraction of that amount and getting it off the books as a potential liability. Most of us don't have that kind of leverage. Both private sector and third sector employees can benefit from the experiences of the public sector, since trends suggest all employment is moving towards the property right concept.

A few public managers or executives in history have sued for wrongful termination, though generally, managers or executives have regarded their employment situation to be "at will" of the governing body. That means that managers or executives serve at the pleasure of the governing body, with all the vagaries that a lack of security implies. But in both the public and private sectors that's changing.

City managers, particularly, have taken the "at will" position largely as a matter of philosophy: The conventional wisdom has been that serving the democratic process is best done if that attitude is taken. Besides missionary work, volunteering for the Peace Corps, and serving the Salvation Army, no other public service career has been so self-sacrificing.

The rest of the world, both public and private, has moved to employee rights faster than a quick-step, Sousa march.

The civil service reforms that were current (just before the council-manager form of government was adopted by the reformers) in the early part of the 20th Century, protected the employees from serving at the will of the patronage supervisors and the elected officials. But to counter the fear that the city manager would have too much power—(the opponents used the word "czar" as the ultimate pejorative), the reformers concluded that the manager needed to have zero job security. So if the manager got too full of himself, he could easily be replaced and that would work to keep him from getting too full of himself.

Over the intervening years, employee rights and protections have increased, but in proportion the manager's have not. Now it's sometimes difficult to discipline a marginal employee until that employee has made many errors of omission and commission, at which point the records begin to be kept more comprehensively until he or she can be removed. There have been many court cases around the country, indicating the employee has a "property right" to the job that cannot be taken away without due process. Discipline becomes more and more an issue like eminent domain.

The manager on the other hand can be terminated upon majority vote of the city council on any given Tuesday. The chief benefit to the city manager over the past twenty years has been the open meetings laws that prohibit a majority of council members from meeting outside those Tuesday sessions.

Some managers or executives serve one city for twenty-five years and then are summarily discharged by a new city council because the new folks think it's "time for a change". Nothing more than that. Not that the incumbent was doing anything wrong, was doing the wrong thing, or wasn't doing enough of anything. Just "time for a change". Twenty-five years. It happens.

Others are fired after six months, when it's discovered that the chemistry that was sensed between the council and manager during the interview process did not continue day in and day out. "Style" is usually the operative word in that situation. It happens.

Some public managers or executives have sued and have won settlements. There are a couple of cases of suits for wrongful termination. One in California and another in Colorado. Most, however, negotiate severance. Those cases that have any chance usually also involve other legal theories. Some of those apply to private positions as well.

In one case the council voted to dismiss the manager for

not taking an action they had directed. They voted to fire him effective immediately and he sued for wrongful termination. After a three and a half week trial, the court ruled in his favor. The Council argued his position was "at will" and since he did not meet their current pleasure, he was dismissed legitimately. His defense was based on the 1980 Tameny case, a claim in tort based on public policy that argues that an individual cannot be dismissed for resisting the performance of illegal acts. That case was supported in a 1992 ruling in Gantt v. Sentry Insurance, which cited the reasoning:

> *An at-will employee possesses a tort action when he or she is discharged for performing an act that public policy would encourage, or for refusing to do something that public policy would condemn...the cases in which violations of public policy are found generally fall into four categories: refusing to violate a statute; performing a statutory obligation; exercising a statutory right or privilege; and reporting an alleged violation of a statute of public importance ...while an at-will employee may be terminated for no reason, or for an arbitrary or irrational reason, there can be no right to terminate for an unlawful reason or a purpose that contravenes fundamental policy.*

This is a good lesson for anyone in the non-profit and for-profit sector as well. Sherron Watkins, the Enron employee who blew the whistle on their accounting practices, the Arthur Anderson vice-president who did similarly, were both acting in the interests of the public and are likely offered some protections. Society could use more such private sector folks coming forward, and I think that message has gotten out to corporate

America. The executive who expects his underlings to go blithely forward carrying his nefarious schemes at the expense of the employee or stockholder is due for a rude comeuppance.

The City of Lakewood, Colorado, terminated their manager one year. He sued under the Section 1983 violation of Civil Rights statute and won a verdict in federal district court in Denver. A subsequent out-of-court settlement was made because legal fees were running too high for the fired manager to sustain the case. Following the judgment, a settlement was reached between the city and plaintiff, and the settlement was sealed. In commenting on the case, Milo Gonzer, Denver attorney for the plaintiff, said, "I don't know why a manager would enter into a contract with any city without talking to me about what to put in the contract. I would have called that new manager in Lakewood, but that's solicitation, and we can't do that."

It's clear that there are examples of improper termination, even of such at-will employees as city managers or executives. Still, the city manager is arguably the most vulnerable public employee outside of the White House staff.

The California League of Municipalities publishes a guide to local government as a baseline document for the newly-elected officials. It deals with wrongful termination issues, among many others. Here's what that document says about wrongful termination, without particular reference to local government managers or executives, and therefore instructive to everyone:

A.   WRONGFUL DISCHARGE/TERMINATION

Tenured (property interest) employees are entitled to be reinstated with back pay if it is ultimately determined by an appellate body or court that the employer did not sustain its burden of establishing good cause for its action. In addition, it may be held that the successful employee is entitled to be reimbursed for his/her attorney's fees and perhaps even to be paid compensatory and possibly punitive money damages.

While at-will employees are normally not legally entitled to be reinstated, they may be entitled to monetary damages if it is determined by a court or jury that the dismissal or other disciplinary action was "wrongful". Common grounds for having actions found to be wrongful are that they violated statutory or constitutional rights, or public policy, or a legal duty of good faith and fair dealing, or involved actions constituting an intentional or negligent infliction of emotional distress.

Two other bases for potential money liability that relate to the disciplinary process are claimed injury resulting from employer responses to requests for references regarding former employees, and claimed damages arising out of the alleged negligent retention of an employee (the "other side of the dismissal coin").

1.   *Violation of Statutory or Constitutional Rights*

When an adverse action is taken against an employee that is held to violate such constitutional rights as free speech, freedom from illegal search, privacy, due process of law and equal protection of the laws, or such statutory rights as engaging in union activities and to be free from employment discrimination, the employer may be found liable for sizable money damage awards. Commonly these are so-called "1983 actions"—that is, actions brought under 42 United States Code Section 1983, being one of the early civil rights laws directed at deprivations of constitutional or statutory rights under color of office.

2. *Violation of Public Policy or the Legal Duty of Good Faith and Fair Dealing*

Assuming no express contractual or statutory provision to the contrary, employment for an indefinite term may be terminated at-will. Such has been the common law rule that is codified in California Labor Code Section 2922. However, under a still evolving series of California court decisions, an employer may nevertheless be found liable in damages for terminating or otherwise taking an adverse action against an at-will employee.

The courts have fashioned three legal theories for finding such liability:

a. By finding an implied contractual commitment to not terminate in the absence of there being good cause. (See earlier 'property interest' discussion).

b. *That the law implies that every contract con-*
    tains a so-called 'covenant of good faith and
    fair dealing', and that a given termination or
    other adverse action violated that covenant.

c. *That a given termination or other adverse*
    action violated public policy (e.g. for protesting
    unsafe working conditions or 'whistleblowing').

   While there still is some legal uncertainty as to
whether these theories for legal damages apply to
public employment, and how limitless a scope of
factual circumstances allow their application ...,
clearly it behooves public employers to establish
and follow notice and communication procedures
that guard against such liability claims.

3. Conduct Constituting Intentional or Negligent Infliction of Emotional Distress

Where the employer engages in extreme and
outrageous conduct that the employer knew, or
should have known, would severely distress the
employee, the employer is answerable in damages.
An example might involve conducting a discipli-
nary investigation in a manner that flagrantly
defames and violates the privacy of the employee.

B.   RESPONSES TO REQUESTS FOR REFERENCES

The former employer's response to a prospective
employer's request for a reference can be the basis for

money damages based on defamation. Generally words that impute to a former employee fraud, dishonesty, misconduct or unfitness for his/her occupation, and that are "published" to a third person, may constitute actionable defamation. However, employers have available certain legal privileges that enable them to communicate such information in a careful and proper manner....

C.   NEGLIGENT HIRING/RETENTION

The law imposes a duty on the employer to use reasonable care to select fit employees and to refrain from retaining unfit employees. This duty (owing the public and fellow employees) not to retain an unfit employee is thus "the other side of the coin" of terminating that employee.

The basis for employer liability in this regard goes beyond the well recognized employer liability for all acts of its employees that are within the course and scope of their employment; here the employer's liability rests on the employers' own negligence, and thus extends to an employee's acts causing damage even though those acts are not within the course and scope of employment (e.g security guard steals, drug counselor sells drugs, mechanic 'joy rides' in customers' cars).

Similarly, an employer is potentially liable for negligent supervision and training of its employees.

California is often referred to by the rest of the country as the land of fruit and nuts, but a large part of that is because California leads in trend-setting, being the first to do something that over time spreads across the country. Prohibiting smoking for example. Encouraging energy conservation, mass transit, health foods, are others. The trends in employment as the California League has provided are trends to be expected to grow nation-wide as well.

IMPLIED CONTRACT

One of the most-used legal theories for wrongful termination is the Employee Manual or Personnel Policy that has been used to describe an "Implied Contract of Continued Employment." When the document says that when you complete a probationary period you then achieve "permanent" status, that has been ruled time and again to be an implied contract committing to a permanent job unless poor job performance is proven. The concept of "permanent" was not intended to mean that, it was used by Human Resource professionals to distinguish between probationary employees and those who have survived the probation. Benefits and other statuses change for many employees after probation, and they become in effect "career employees." The employee on probation is often considered to have no rights and may be terminated for no reason at all. Some supervisors treat the employee on probation as one who has no rights, and if they don't demonstrate the ability to do the job in one or two months, they're toast. The better approach to probation is to consider it a period to help the employee learn how to do the job. Cutting them loose prior to completion of probation is bad human resource management, in my judgment. It costs too much to recruit, check background, interview, and select to not give the employee finally making it through the process the opportunity to learn what is expected and how to do the job. If they haven't done it by the sixth month, then consider letting them go. Also consider extending probation. There is much invested in getting the new employee to this point. To cut them loose after a month or two is just plain arrogance and power being wielded, and the supervisor who does that needs to be scrutinized.

CONTRACT TERMS

*"The first thing we do,
Let's kill all the lawyers."*
—Dick, Henry VI

Most managerial contracts discuss a term of three years or so, but take care not to imply that the contract is a "no cut" or that there are property rights vested in the contract for the entire term. Many states have a disclaimer in the authorizing statute that prohibits a contract for a public manager to extend beyond the term of the current governing body, or some such limit.

That's in contrast to the school superintendents' contracts, whose terms often extend for five years or more, all of the compensation to be paid if termination occurs. Academic freedom is often cited. For the city manager, it's more accepted that he or she is a part of government, while the school superintendent is not. I don't know. Why the administrative head of a governmental agency is not thought to be part of government is beyond me. But the distinction is interesting. Major league sports coaches also have great contracts. You wonder about the sense of the owners who give a baseball manager a five year contract for a million bucks a year, knowing that he's got a dog of a roster, knowing that the only good guys are free agents in one or two years. They are therefore assured that performance will be mediocre at best and fans will demand a firing, and the owner will pay the guy for the full five years. But then everything else major league baseball does makes you wonder about the owners. Who wouldn't want that contract, though.

SAMPLE EMPLOYMENT AGREEMENT

Appendix B shows a sample employment agreement. It is not being recommended as the best, or a standard, or something that fits you. Only you can know that. Employment agreements are not one-size-fits-all; they are unique, one-of-a-kind documents for you and the hiring authority. This example of an employment agreement does have a termination clause along the lines of those currently being negotiated. It is suggested you consider it in your deliberations about your agreement.

FLAGMAN AS FALLBACK

*"When you're throwin' your weight around,
be ready to have it thrown around by somebody else."*
—Will Rogers

⸺

Howard Willingham was one of my early mentors. I learned a great deal from him, and as with all mentors some of it was learning how to do right and some was an object lesson on what to avoid. One of Howard's early pieces of advice was offered while we were driving to Dallas one summer. As we were stopped by the flagman protecting the construction workers and waited in a line of cars on the highway for the paving project to allow us to proceed, he offered his own fallback position advice. He said, "Remember, you can always get a job as a Flagman." I didn't think much of the advice at the time, but the need to have a fallback position in mind is a point well-taken.

Howard was a bulldog manager. The Bulldog was bred over generations, before our current sensibilities were refined, to attack a bull in the bullring by grabbing the bull's nose and hanging on while the bull swung it around and tried to dislodge it. When Howard sank his teeth into a problem, he didn't let go until it or he was done in. Usually he solved the problem and made things work much better. But like a bulldog, he sometimes didn't realize that what he had ahold of was bigger and stronger and very dangerous.

Howard created a major water project in Texarkana. He combined several cities into a water supply compact that improved the use of water in the entire area significantly. That made possible the attraction of a major employer, a water-intensive paper mill with about four hundred jobs. But in the process he attacked a sizable cadre of good ol' boys who were involved in the water business at the time. Howard affected their play-toy.

In turn they went after his city council, got them defeated, and a new group elected. Howard resigned that next day, effective when the new folks were to be seated. Then the old group gave Howard a two-year consulting contract on water-related issues, at just about his last salary.

At this point, Howard had a fallback position that was pretty fair. But he was probably also following the third rule of politics that says, Don't get mad, Get even. The problem is that it can be destructive.

Howard wasn't satisfied with his contract. He organized an African-American enclave of homes near the paper mill to incorporate into a city, with the understanding that this new City of Dominoe would grant him a liquor license. He would have a liquor store on the main road to the paper mill, and in turn he would hire local residents and contribute funds to the community center. The liquor store would be the only one between the Arkansas line and Dallas.

A year or so after that Howard was found beaten to death. No one was ever charged.

I often think of Howard when I see a Flagman on a highway project. And I know the bulldog got a piece of whoever came after him.

But I suppose the lesson from the story is that you can go too far in getting even, and the second rule of politics is that All Things That Go Around, Come Around. So, the admonition of the Shift Commander on the TV show *Hill Street Blues* is sound: "Be careful out there."

CHAPTER 4

Financial Specifics

"If you fail to plan you have a plan for failure":
—Innumerable Investment Sales Folk

—⊗⊗⊗—

KNOWING BENEFITS IS A FALLBACK POSITION IN ITSELF

In working through this book, people will gain an understanding of what their situation is, just in case they find themselves in some trouble with their hiring authority. Knowing where you are and where you will be at any given point in time is a great help to peace of mind. And peace of mind has beneficent effects upon keeping a good relationship with that hiring authority.

David Geller, a financial advisor to high net-worth individuals, offers good tips for those who are no longer employed. If he needs to give advice to high-net-worth clients, then the rest of us need to pay attention.

> **Money-Management Tips For Laid-Off Professionals**
> *Among the top concerns after a job loss is the ability to pay bills and make ends meet until you find a new job. Fear*

and stress can impede the capacity of even level-headed people to think clearly about their financial situation. But proper planning can relieve some of the strain and anxiety during this time of uncertainty.

One of the first things you'll want to do is rein in your expenses. When Nicole Lipson was laid off earlier this year, a look at her household cash flow showed that her second largest expense, after her mortgage payment, is childcare. The Atlanta-based marketing professional is considering moving her children from an expensive private day care facility to a public-school-based program for two days per week. But she's waiting a month before making any changes.

"I can save $200 a month doing this alone, much more if I made the change long term. While my kids aren't thrilled with the prospect of the school program full time, two days a week is very tolerable," she says.

"Losing your job and assessing your expenses can be a real eye-opener," says Todd Mark, public-relations coordinator for the Atlanta office of Consumer Credit Counseling Service, a nonprofit organization that provides free budget counseling and debt-management plans. He speaks from experience, having been laid off in February from a job as producer of a consumer talk-radio show. "It makes you more conscientious about how you spend and save your money," he says.

Besides tightening your budget, you can take other steps to better manage your finances after you've been laid off. Considering the following tips may help you make the right decisions.

1. Negotiate with your former employer. Most companies do their best to develop a fair severance package. However, there's often room for negotiation.

When you're offered severance, ask questions and focus on understanding your options, says Bob Lewis, general manager of the Atlanta office of Lee Hecht Harrison, an outplacement and career development firm based in Woodcliff Lake, N.J. "Don't react with your emotions," he says. Ask how much time you have by law to respond, and take 24 to 48 hours to make any decisions.

Mr. Mark received six weeks' pay in a lump-sum check and was allowed to exercise his stock options, but says he now wishes he knew the size of average severance packages because he would have felt justified asking for more. "I was so dumbfounded by what had happened, I was just happy to have any severance," he says.

While companies don't owe you additional severance benefits, they may be open to negotiating with you, Mr. Lewis says. When approaching your employer, choose the one or two items on your list that are most important to you. You're more likely to get what you want if you're not expecting every possible concession.

According to Lee Hecht Harrison, there's no universal standard for severance pay. Some companies may offer one to four weeks for each year of service. Other companies will provide those employed longer than three months a typical minimum of four to six weeks. You may be offered a lump-sum payment, but if you ask to receive your severance payments on the same schedule as your normal paychecks, you may be able to continue your health-insurance benefits during this time as well.

Other points that could be negotiated:

- *If you're due an annual bonus, the company may be able to give you a prorated amount. If you're asked to stay on with your employer more than two weeks after your layoff notification, consider asking for a stay bonus.*

- *If you're due stock options, ask for an accelerated vesting period so you can exercise them now. "There's no reason to leave money on the table," says Mr. Lewis.*

- *If you're close to retirement age, you can ask the company to enhance your pension plan or deferred-compensation plan by applying credit, on a one-time basis, in the form of years of age and/or years of service. The formula for being fully vested in such plans varies by company but often is some combination of your age and the number of years you've worked there.*

- *Consider asking to keep your office space and phone line while you job hunt. If you have a company car, you might be able to buy it at a steep discount. Your desktop or laptop computer might be yours for free, if you ask for it. Additionally, remember to ask for job-search assistance from a reputable corporate outplacement firm.*

- *Companies typically are willing to give more than they initially offer to avoid wrongful-firing lawsuits and to maintain a positive image with remaining employees. Consider consulting with an employment attorney to make sure your rights haven't been violated.*

2. Keep covered. *Consider your health-care insurance options, such as getting on your spouse's plan, which probably is your least costly option, or applying to the* **Consolidated Omnibus Budget Reconciliation Act (COBRA)** *program, which will allow for at least 18 months of coverage at lower, group rates.*

Mr. Mark purchased health insurance for his family as individuals from Blue Cross Blue Shield for $305 per month. "It was surprisingly inexpensive," says Mr. Mark.

Make sure your life-insurance coverage is adequate to meet your family's needs. It may cost less than you think to provide a blanket of security for your family. Term-insurance costs have come down dramatically during the past decade.

3. Make a list of what's coming in and what's going out. *Take a realistic look at your family's other income and overall expenses. But don't make drastic changes to your lifestyle right away.*

Mr. Mark and his wife had set aside a nine-month emergency fund for unexpected expenses, "so I didn't panic," he says. "I was able to consider all my options, and I didn't take the first job offer that came along." In the meantime, they cut back on discretionary expenses such as dining out and entertainment. Within a month, he'd found his new position.

Try not to panic when considering additional funds. For example, you don't want to sell your stocks right away for the extra cash you might not need.

4. Apply for unemployment benefits. There's no stigma in receiving these payments. Companies are required to pay into the fund. "It's your due. Frankly, the money comes in handy for expenses like groceries," Ms. Lipson says.

Mr. Mark filed immediately. "Many people reminded me that this was my tax dollars at work and that I would be a fool not to," he says. As it turned out, Mr. Mark wasn't eligible for six weeks, the length of his severance pay, and he found a new job after four weeks.

But be warned: Unemployment benefits are taxable. So you won't get stuck owing Uncle Sam back taxes next April, have federal and state taxes (if applicable) deducted automatically.

5. Consider applying for a home-equity loan. If you own your home and are still employed, you may want to apply for a home-equity loan. You may need the extra money when you get laid off, and it's difficult to get a line of credit without a job.

6. Reduce your systematic savings. Many people contribute money on a regular basis to investments such as mutual funds. But if you're laid off and money is tight, consider suspending these payments until you find a new job.

Mr. Mark stopped all his monthly contributions. He didn't, however, touch his investments. "Though my job situation changed, my retirement plans and investment strategies did not," he says.

7. Don't raid your 401(k). *It's often tempting when you lose a job to withdraw money from your 401(k) or retirement plan. Don't do it. Distributions from qualified retirement plans before age 59 1/2 generally are subject to income taxes and a 10% penalty. More importantly, the money you take out won't have the chance to grow and help provide for a secure retirement.*

However, there are situations, called "hardship withdrawals," available to 401(k) owners that avoid the 10% penalty on withdrawals made before age 59 1/2. Generally, these exceptions are limited to an immediate financial need, says Sheldon J. Donner, tax partner with the Atlanta-based accounting firm Donner, Weiser & Rosenberg P.C. These include medical expenses for you, your spouse or dependent; the purchase of a residence; payment of tuition, fees, room and board for the next 12 months for post-secondary education; and to prevent eviction or foreclosure

8. Decide which bills to pay first. *Falling behind on your mortgage will lead to late penalties and could cost you your home, so this payment should be first on your list. You need heat and lights, so utility bills come next. Since you need transportation to find a job, keep up your car payments.*

"A big mistake people make is to pay the bill whose collectors are the most harassing," says Mr. Mark. If the choice is either-or, never pay an unsecured debt such as a credit card before paying a secured debt, such as your house or car, he adds.

9. Reduce credit-card interest rates. *Call your credit-card company and explain your situation in a courteous manner. Assure the representative that you're actively seeking a new job. If you have a good payment history, be sure to mention it. Ask to have your interest charges waived for a few months or at least reduced. If you've incurred late fees, request that they be waived.*

"You have nothing to lose — except high interest rates," says Mr. Mark.

You also can try another tack. Ms. Lipson couldn't get a better rate on the main card she uses most often, so she applied for another account with a low introductory rate. She moved half her old balance to the new card and makes the minimum payment on it. "On the other, I still pay a little more than minimum and have reduced specialty shopping to as close to zero as possible," she says.

— Mr. Geller is chief executive officer of Atlanta-based GV Financial Advisors, a registered investment advisor and financial-planning firm serving private business owners, high-income professionals and high-net-worth individuals.

COBRA AND HEALTH INSURANCE

The current law provides that your last employer, if there are 20 or more employees and there is health coverage, must provide you with the opportunity to continue your health insurance group coverage, at your expense, for 18 months after you terminate employment. And another 12 months under certain conditions. You have to pay the actuarial cost, the amount that is not subsidized by your employer.

Usually you have to let the employer know that you want

the coverage and make arrangements for payment within sixty days of leaving to be eligible.

There are state laws that apply to companies that aren't subject to Cobra and you may be eligible for those. Check with your state insurance office. There's also a website that provides useful information. It's **www.insure.com/health/cobra3.html.**

There are other choices. You can get reasonably-priced individual policies if you have no major health issues and you can join independent groups for group policies. The National Association for the Self-employed is one such group offering health insurance plans. There is also short-term medical coverage, ranging from 30 days to six months with reduced coverage, becoming almost a Major Medical plan, not covering office visits.

IRA AND PENSION FUNDS

Most financial advisors suggest taking a lump sum distribution upon leaving an employer, including stock options if you have them, and rolling them over into a self-directed IRA. But consult your financial advisor. You usually have 60 days to roll a lump sum into a new IRA.

UNEMPLOYMENT COMPENSATION

We've already touched on this earlier under the heading Termination Agreement. However, some points bear further discussion. Eligibility for unemployment may depend in your state upon how the termination is characterized. For "cause" is usually the determining factor for eligibility, Kiplinger's Personal Finance magazine reports. If you haven't been fired for cause and you worked four of the last five quarters, you probably qualify, they say. The agencies handling unemployment compensation also have made it much easier to apply. Thirty-three states allow you to apply over the phone, 16 states allow you to do so online. Check the details at the website of the National Association of Workforce Agencies: www.workforceatm.org.

Kiplinger's research says the average unemployment benefit is $200 a week across the country. But in California if you earned "more than $9,504 in your highest earning quarter within the last 18 months, you could qualify for $330 a week." Massachusetts' maximum benefit is $512 a week.

Whether you want to apply for unemployment comp now or later can well be affected by what happens during the termination. That's a personal decision dealing with values and financial needs. Dealing with it upfront as part of a fallback position is important to how you act when the termination happens.

GET ADVICE FROM PROFESSIONALS

This is also discussed in more detail earlier. Just to reiterate, at the time of termination, we all need more help than we know. Get advice from a lawyer and an accountant, particularly about the termination agreement. Beyond that, counseling is a good way to get your mind back together; it may be difficult to confide in a spouse all the fears and worries that would be more easily related to a professional counselor.

SOCIAL SECURITY

If you have forty quarters of work under social security,

with recorded contributions, then you have full social security benefits. That's ten years of work with social security contributions made.

Social security doesn't do much for you in case of unemployment. But it needs to be built into your financial analysis equation, because if retirement contributions are a concern to you, and you wonder how to keep preparing for retirement during unemployment, it's good to know where you sit with social security.

For disability benefits you need to have 39 quarters and 20 of those need to have occurred in the last 10 years.

The Social Security Administration now sends out statements of eligibility qualification annually. But if you haven't received one, you can write or call the Social Security Administration (1-800-772-1213) to obtain a copy of your statement and find the number of quarters they have recorded for eligibility.

If you haven't received it in the past three years, you should get it now. It's a good part of your preparation.

HOW LONG WILL YOUR MONEY LAST? MORE MAKING IT LAST CALCULATIONS

Vanguard did an analysis of how much money can be taken from assets annually and still make them last. They suggest there are three approaches to figuring that out.

The first is a plan to spend a little principal and the income. This table shows how much can be withdrawn and spent annually based on how much is earned as income.

HOW LONG WILL YOUR ASSETS LAST												
Annual Withdrawl Rate	Average total return											
	4%	5%	6%	7%	8%	9%	10%	11%	12%	13%	14%	15%
15	7	8	8	9	9	10	11	12	14	16	20	
14	8	9	9	10	11	11	13	14	17	21		
13	9	9	10	11	12	13	15	17	22			
12	10	11	11	12	14	16	18	23				
11	11	12	13	14	16	19	25					
10	13	14	15	17	20	26						
9	14	16	18	22	28							
8	17	20	23	30								
7	21	25	33									
6	28	36										

That table shows that if you invest your money at 6% and take 15% of it out annually, your money will last 8 years. If you take out only 10% of your money while it is earning 6%, the money will last 15 years. And if you only take 7% a year of your total and have it at 6%, the money will last 33 years.

The 4% scenario is a second plan. It was developed by Harvard and suggests that you set up your assets as half in stocks and half in bonds and cash and then take out 4% of the total portfolio value the first year and then increase the dollar amount taken out the next year by the first year's inflation rate. And if you continue that year by year, your money should last in perpetuity barring some catastrophic ruin of the economy. You don't need perpetuity. You only need to avoid some catastrophic ruin of the economy. How to do that is beyond the scope of this text.

HOW LONG WILL YOU LIVE?

You also need to figure out how long you'll live, and how long your spouse will live, needing support. Actuaries figure all that out using complex formulas that are very conservative. They too play the odds, and they want to err on the safe side, so some pension fund doesn't run out of money before it runs out of pensioners. So they figure you're likely to live longer than you are. That's because on average, they can figure your length of life, from wherever you are now. It won't be accurate for you, but it will be for your age group. Half of them will live longer and half will die sooner. On average, they are correct about you.

That's like the story about the three actuaries who went duck hunting. A lone Mallard flew over their blind and the first actuary shot and they could all see he shot in front of the duck. The second actuary shot and it was clear he was behind the duck. All three of them high-fived each other and said, "Got him!" The duck flew on, undoubtedly thankful the hunters were actuaries.

The *American Funds Investor* cited government estimates of length of life, based on actuarial calculations. They say that a 65-year old man can expect to live about 16 years and a 65-year old woman can expect to live about 19 years. They add, "some financial advisers add 10 years or more for conservatism. Others suggest inflation-protected income to age 100."

Here's an actuarial table the *American Funds Investor* suggests for the length of time your age group will live:

If You Currently Are	Your Age Group Will Live This Long	
	Men	Women
45	76.8	81.3
50	77.5	81.8
55	78.3	82.3
60	78.9	83.1
65	80.9	84.2
70	82.9	85.7
75	84.9	87.1
80	87.8	88.8
85	90.5	91.6
TILT		

CHAPTER 5

Things to Do Right Away in Your Profession

"The deepest principle in human nature is the craving to be appreciated."
—William James

———

EXECUTIVE RECRUITERS

Executive Recruiters, or "headhunters," have come into their own in all professions. The large number of people in the job market makes the selection process complicated and time-consuming and the litigious society makes fair and careful handling of personnel a necessity. The trend toward downsizing thrusts ever-greater numbers of private sector managers or executives into the market, and one consequence of the peace dividend's military base closures is competition from former military officers. So the use of executive recruiters is a growing trend, not a shrinking one.

THEY NEED YOU AND YOU NEED THEM

Many people say they don't like working with headhunters.

When they are queried they explain this dislike in one of two ways: (1) they feel that the recruiter stands in-between them and the hiring authority, which is uncomfortable and maybe unnatural; and (2) they believe that the recruiters don't like them or don't take them as a recommended candidate to the good jobs.

Others have no problems with working with recruiters, feeling that the headhunters help define the job for the hiring authority and clarify issues for the candidates. My experience is the latter: recruiters learn about the elements of the job that are critical and the character of the hiring authority, and that information is extremely useful in evaluating "fit" between the candidate and the organization.

Some recruiters are perceived by managers or executives to have their "in-ys" and "out-ys", as one jobseeker expressed it. Those who are favored and are touted to hiring authorities are the "in-ys" and those who are not are the "out-ys." That likely has a lot to do with the applicant's interview style and management style, and the expectations of the hiring body. One recruiter, who wishes to remain anonymous says, "Frankly, some (people) have not brushed up on their interview skills in some time. To take them to a (hiring authority) is to embarrass myself professionally." Another says there are "managers or executives out there who are out of touch with what hiring authorities want in terms of participation in the decision-making process: to take one of those to the hiring authority is to invite the deadly criticism that I didn't listen".

The business of recruiting is one of "finding 'fits' between parties," another recruiter defines. "We may have 30 to 50 applicants for a good job. We winnow and narrow, looking for the best fit all the time. Then we take a recommended sample to the hiring body, in a process that's agreed upon in advance. Some boards want two dozen referrals and then they want to narrow to the 6 or so they want to interview. Others want 8 or 10 and to narrow from there. The recruiter needs to provide the service the hiring authority wants."

"After all," another says, "there is no one true way of doing this. Nothing works all the time."

The criticism about "in-ys" and "out-ys" is one the recruiters work at countering. But some managers or executives feel, as one has said, that "a manager has to hire a recruiter to hire a department head to be one on the 'inside' of that firm." I don't know of any correlation studies run by anyone to see if there is any connection, but a number of managers or executives have indicated that they feel that way about specific firms.

The firms try to avoid being preferential. "Face it," one says, "we can't survive if we are preferential: while managers or executives jobs are turning over with greater frequency, we can't make a living by taking the same circle of people to those jobs." It's up to the manager to make the contacts with the recruiting firms early and often.

CONTACT MAINTENANCE

"You Can't Make Friends When You Need Them"
—Gerry Horak

───❧───

Whether you're in the sales business, getting a grant from a foundation, or just running an organization that has to hire folks from time to time, it's important to make frequent contact with relevant personnel. In today's world, that kind of contact maintenance is essential with recruiters in your field. A former advisor of mine suggested "You can't make friends when you need them." It's a salesman's mantra, but it fits the world of competition that the recruiter deals in. Each manager or executive needs to know the recruiters, and they need to know each executive. Not just personally, but in terms of professional achievements as well.

Recruiters watch publications for mentions of innovations and successes. Some managers or executives keep in touch by sending materials to recruiters, saying "I'm not really looking, but if something is out there for professional advancement, I have had these experiences and you might keep me in mind." Recruiters appreciate that "tickle" of their memory.

One manager of my acquaintance admitted she occasionally submits a resume and an application for a position for which she isn't really interested. "The drill is good for me," she says, "but most importantly it causes the recruiter to take a serious look at my background and experience." On occasion she has been persuaded to go to the interview because there was such a good fit. In sharing her comment around, I've heard from several managers or executives who say that that's not a bad strategy. One said, "We don't know all the organizations around, in which we might like to work, and the best way to check them out is with a recruiter." A recruiter says, "Part of my job is to attract those who are otherwise not interested. If a manager is using the process to continue contact, that's fine. We sell to each other."

Norm Roberts, formerly of Norm Roberts Associates, and

now with DMG Maximus, Inc., in reviewing this text, cautioned that people should not submit materials for positions they really aren't serious about. That would "burn a lot of time" of the search firm. So if you intend to "tickle" his memory, he suggests it be done sparingly.

SYZYGY IN THE RELATIONSHIP

Recruiters readily will admit that they are more comfortable taking someone who is a known quantity in an interview to a hiring authority than someone they don't know well. How will he or she respond to a stress interview? If someone on the interview panel doesn't address sensitive issues well, how will the applicant react? The test of performance for the recruiter is how well the hiring authority likes the candidates presented.

"Some employers want to look at diverse styles," Jerry Oldani, of The Oldani Group, says. "They aren't sure if they want to replace their last executive with a clone or with a contrast. Others know exactly and want to pick from a litter of like pups."

Whichever is the case, the recruiter will explain the approach the employer is taking and why you are being presented. It makes the recruiter happy when you connect with the hiring authority and deliver a product he or she can be proud of having presented. Then it's likely the recruiter will take you again. In this sense then, the relationship is mutually supportive. Each needs the other for success. When the two are working together for each other's success, then synergy sets in, the whole is greater than the sum of the parts, and the parts are the candidate and the recruiter serving each other well. That's a perfect alignment, what I call a Syzygy.

Recruiter Norman Roberts adds, "The initial test of performance of the recruiter is how the employer likes the candidate." He points out that "...disclosure needs to be complete. There must be no surprises." That means there must be absolutely no serious concealed infractions: DUI's, sexual harassment charges, whatever. "Recruiters can deal with a lot of things, but not the unknown." He advises that the candidate needs to "treat the recruiter like a therapist or an attorney. Recruiters need to know all the facts in order to be an advocate for the candidate."

To that end, like the press pulling the clippings on past positions, he does the same thing. Then he quizzes the candidate: What are we going to find? Roberts calls that "vaccinating the client."

Roberts says due diligence requirements now make the job much more difficult than when he got involved in 1969, but it's a much better process now.

Recruiter Bob Murray, of Bob Murray Associates, says that in the past the manager ethic suggested "a manager wasn't a manager until he had been fired." There was a feeling that being fired comes with the territory. Murray says if that were ever true, he does not find it true now. "It is a difficulty that has to be dealt with. Elected officials wonder about a candidate who was fired." This applies even in the case of ethical concerns. In his experience, one manager was fired for not doing what council asked, when the manager thought the action was unethical. "Nevertheless," Murray said, "bosses of any kind have trouble sympathizing with an employee who doesn't do what the boss asks."

He advises that managers or executives have many obligations, including "an obligation not to be thrown out on the street."

MANAGERS OR EXECUTIVES
ARE LIKE RAZOR BLADES

"Managers or executives must resolve to lead,
Not merely to manage."
—Warren Bennis

———∞∞∞———

Dr. Bill Mathis does a good deal of work in organizational development and works with city councils and non-profit boards, helping to evaluate managers or executives and executive directors. So he works to try to make the organization work with the executive and then he helps the executive work with the governing body. He came to this niche after working several years as a counselor in prisons. With great restraint we eschew the obvious opportunity to make a correlation between prisoners and governing bodies. He offers this observation about city councils, and their view of managers or executives being interchangeable, almost all alike. He says they feel that managers or executives are like razors, "One will give you just about as good a shave as another." Editorial writers have sometimes also fallen into the trap of assuming that any manager would do the same thing as any other. The *Eureka Times Standard* once editorialized about hiring a local boy over one from another state and city, stating that the latter would bring a "cookie cutter approach to a city," doing the same things over and over again, from one city to the next. This displayed an horrific ignorance of the role of a manager in assessing what an organization needs, and then providing it. True, some managers or executives get a reputation for being a one-trick pony, with a specialty in layoffs, or some other cookie cutter cost reducing tactic. That happens in the private sector as well as the public and non-profit, as we've seen earlier with Al Dunlap.

The perception, however, of such interchangeability between managers or executives makes it geometrically more difficult to get over even a minor smudge on your record, as Norm Roberts indicated.

MULTIPLE INTERVIEW GAUNTLET: ALTERNATIVE SELECTION MECHANISM

"Don't measure with a micrometer and then hack it off with an axe."
—Tom Lee

The process of selection is so difficult today, yet so important, that many companies and agencies are using multiple interviews to find the flaws in candidates and weed out those that won't fit in. It's another form of stress interview, to have you go through a series of interviews. But it happens. It is widespread in the public sector for high profile positions, and it's growing in the private sector.

Whatever device is used, whether public, private, or non-profit, there has to be a relationship between employee and boss and nothing beats getting to know each other by face to face contact over a period of time.

JOB ROAD MAPPING

*"If you don't set goals,
you can't regret not reaching them."*
—Yogi Berra

Richard Hughes wrote the book **Put Your Best Foot Forward,** in which he provides practical advice on every aspect of job search, from digging around to find a job through the interview and salary negotiation. One of his concepts he calls "job road mapping." (The book uses a good deal of automobile metaphors.) He says you "need a job road map to keep your job advancement, improvement, or (in these traumatic times with layoffs) survival activities in focus." That makes great sense and fits with the thesis of this book. He then proceeds to tell us how to "discover the eight truths" of a job road map, by writing down answers to his eight questions as they apply to you:

1. **In what geographic location would you like to work? Why?**

2. **In what specific kind of industry, profession, or occupation do you want to work? Why?**

3. **In what specific kind of organization do you want to work (e.g. size, corporate culture)? Why?**

4. **What types of work do you like to do? Why?**

5. **At what types of work are you good? Why?**

6. **What kinds of people do you like to work for and with? Why?**

7. What specific kind of position do you want? Why?

8. What sacrifices are you willing to make to get where you want to go?

Mr. Hughes suggests that what this exercise will do for you is let you know "what you really want with regard to location, occupation, types and characteristics of employers and positions." It will also provide insight into "how well what you like to do matches up against what you are good at doing." Finally, it will reveal to you the "kinds of sacrifices you are willing to endure to get where you want to go."

This allows you to have an individual and unique job road map. He suggests you "not automatically pick up or follow road maps already available or ones you have used in the past."

Hughes is showing us that we have to take charge of ourselves and our careers. As Peter Drucker has advised, "The only things that evolve by themselves in an organization are disorder, friction, and malperformance." It's also true for the individual: your career has to be managed and directed.

—∞∞∞—

CHAPTER 6

Things to Do Right Away if You're Fired: Personal

"They've done us a favor":
—Spouse of a fired manager

———— ✤ ————

RECOGNIZE THAT OTHERS HAVE HANDLED IT: SO CAN YOU

Many have been through a forced transition, and almost all have survived. The consensus is that most have been better for the experience. Think about the other things that can happen in a life: losing a spouse, a child, major illness. This termination is not life threatening. It's difficult, but on the lifetime stress scale, it's at the low end. You can handle it.

Sure, it's a blow to your self-esteem. And self-esteem is what gives you confidence, and confidence is necessary for a leader and for decision-making. A suggested self-esteem building protocol is a simple mantra you repeat over and over to yourself: "I'm happy. I'm healthy. I feel terrific." Another is the subliminal message reportedly inserted in white noise in department stores to prevent shoplifting. It says, "My mother loves me."

RECOGNIZE YOU ARE
SUPPORTING YOUR VALUES

*"Values come from where you were when,
and what happened then."*
—Mathias

Some time ago I decided to leave a position after confronting the foxhole companions I was dealing with. A good friend heard about my decision and called. He was solicitous and supportive and emphasized that I was "living my values." We discussed the fact that as executives we were prepared for termination, following the philosophy that the organization is sometimes best served by the governing body's seeking a manager more in tune with its own perceived philosophy.

The realization that you are living your values makes the whole experience easier. Not easy, but easier.

SPOUSE COMMUNICATION

*"Oh, what a tangled web do parents weave,
When they think that their children are naïve."*
—Ogden Nash

Anytime we have a problem as severe as losing a job, communication on the home front is imperative. Spouse and children need to be talked to and involved. With all the layoffs and downsizing actions occurring lately, more and more psychologists are exhorting those involved to communicate with the children as well as the spouse. But certainly the communication process begins with the spouse.

50,000 WORDS A DAY

Dr. David Morrison is a psychiatrist who is a teacher of life, humanity, and adjustment to stress. Many have attended his courses or heard him speak while he was working out of the Menninger Clinic, teaching stress management and human understanding. He said the biggest problem in families is that members get out of sync with individual desires to listen and desires to speak. That is, he said, a husband wants to talk while a wife doesn't—or perhaps more commonly in today's job world—just the reverse.

According to Morrison, psychological studies indicate that the average human being has a need to speak 50,000 words per day. Any less and the psyche is in deficit and must verbalize to someone. Any more, and overload exists; the psyche just wants to shut down and rest.

Morrison's example is of the man who comes home from his job in some leadership position (leadership being invariably verbal); he's had to communicate his thoughts all day, and to a variety of listeners. He's probably expended 75,000 to 100,000 words that day trying to communicate to his bosses or co-workers why they need to do what he suggests to get to the end that he feels will be success.

For his rest and regeneration, he wants to shut down, "veg out" in front of the TV, where no thinking has to go on. There, he can watch a Western in which all the plots and possible endings are known, so that curiosity is only challenged about how the characters get to the end. Or he can watch a football game in which, again, only a couple of endings are possible, but the route to the end is of some interest.

He doesn't have to predict the ends or the means, and he doesn't have to justify to doubters—or to himself—that he knows what he's talking about. He encounters a wife who has left a career for a few years, while the children are young. She's been home with them all day, and she's used about 1,250 adult words. She has a deficit of about 49,000 words, while he's overloaded by 25,000 words. She needs to talk to him—and have him listen and react—while he wants to turn his mind off.

She can't wait for him to get home and have some adult conversation. So when he walks in the door, she wants to start.

So what happens?

Most likely, neither meets the other's needs. One or both is unhappy unless they both understand and try to meet the verbal needs of the other. Unless they try to satisfy each other's intellectual needs. Unless they know that another day the roles will be reversed, and the needs and supports also will be reversed.

The poet Rick Masten illustrates the point as he describes the changing roles of men and women in families. He said that at about the age of forty, the man has had it with his career, and he comes home one day, throws his hat in the closet, and says, "It ain't out there." At the same time, the wife has just gotten the kids through school and is resuming her own career, so she's putting on her hat and saying, "The hell it ain't."

There's probably little conflict beyond money and sex that is as significant as the difference in needs and capacities of family partners to be a listener at the right time.

Clearly, the time of job separation is one of the best times to hear each other.

STRESS REDUCTION: LIGHTEN UP

"I laugh because I must not cry.
That is all.
That is all."

—A. Lincoln

"He who laughs, lasts"

—Mary Pettibone Poole

———————

C.W. Metcalf is a humorist, lecturer, and co-author of ***Lighten Up: Survival Skills for People Under Pressure.*** He teaches people how to cope with stress through humor. He says, "Humor is a set of survival skills that relieve tension...in the face of relentless change."

As Metcalf says, "The first humor skill is the ability to see the absurdity in difficult situations, the second humor skill is the ability to take yourself lightly while taking your work seriously, and the third humor skill is a disciplined sense of joy in being alive."

He came to that wisdom while working with Hospice, in of course the most humorless of situations. As he worked with folks who were terminally ill, he knew that courage had an abiding sense of humor. Metcalf has taken his message to major corporations suffering bankruptcy, layoffs, and closings. We all can benefit from the perspective of humor.

"If you lose the power to laugh,
you lose the power to think."

—Clarence Darrow

DEALING WITH THE LITTLE DEATH
OR ANY OTHER GRIEF

Termination is considered by the psychologist Magruder a "little death," and needs to be treated as such. Grief counselors after the 9.11.01 disaster were at the forefront of discussion on how to deal with death. Here's what Alan Bavley wrote in the **Kansas City Star** that the grief counselors say:

- *"Recall other times you've experienced strong emotions and how you handled them."*

- *"Don't compare yourself to others; everyone deals with stress in different ways."*

- *"Get plenty of rest."*

- *"Get continuous exercise. Don't let up. It's a stress-reducer."*

- *"Continue to eat well and avoid excessive drinking."*

- *"Talk to someone you trust and can confide in."*

- *"Do something to make a contribution: give blood, volunteer help, collect materials of use, find a way to be of service."*

- *"Do something that makes you feel like you're in some degree of control. Enjoy your life."*

- *"If strong feelings won't go away, seek professional help."*

THE ULTIMATE STRESS REDUCTION IS A FALLBACK PLAN

Fallback Position is the ultimate stress reduction tool. If you know what you're going to do and know your situation, you know you can cope with whatever happens. Stress mainly comes from not knowing "what if." Our minds can conjure all sorts of ills and fates, but we aren't certain at all times that we can handle them with the style and grace that we display in our professional lives.

TIME MANAGEMENT AS STRESS REDUCTION

One of Parkinson's laws was that "Work expands to fill the time available." It could include any activity, not just work. As the recently retired will attest, you can spend the morning reading the day's newspaper if that's all you have to do. And if it's what you want to do, that's fine. But if you're recently fired or laid off, you probably want to spend the majority of your time in a productive search for another job. And you are somewhat stressed that it is taking longer than you thought it would. You are worried about the money, and worried that you might have to deplete savings or cut into your retirement account for living expenses.

Using the principles of time management can help reduce that stress and worry, because they show you that you're being smart, you're doing the important things first, and that will pay off eventually.

Those techniques are written in many books, and they suggest in various ways and under different systems that the most important things get attention first, that each is attended to in order, and then the next and so on. As Major Winchester in the MASH series said in his introductory surgery, "I do one thing—very, very, well—and then I move on." He was corrected that the MASH unit did "meatball" surgery in a triage system to save as many lives as was possible. Stephen Covey's system of categorization of the process is to create a Time Management Matrix that defines the Important and distinguishes that from the merely Urgent. It looks like this:

URGENT VS. IMPORTANT		
	URGENT	**NOT URGENT**
Important	*I. Activities*	*II. Activities*
	Crises	Prevention
	Pressing Problems	Relationship Building
	Deadline-driven Projects	Recognizing New Opportunities
Not Important	*III. Activities*	*IV. Activities*
	Interruptions, Calls	Trivia, Busy Work
	Some Mail, Some Reports	Some Mail
	Some Meetings	Some Phone Calls
	Pressing Matters	Time Wasters
	Popular Activities	Pleasant Activities

Many advisers suggest making a list of the things to do tomorrow at the end of each day, prioritizing those by an A, B, C designation. In ***Time Is Money, Save It,*** Siewert says this:

- *"The A tasks are most important. 15% of our tasks are in this group but their value in terms of contribution to goal achievement is 65%.*

- *"The B tasks make up 20% of the total and their contribution is 20%.*

- *"The C tasks of less importance make up 65% of the total but only 15% of the value of management tasks."*

If you follow these practices you will know you're doing the most important things first for getting that new job, but you'll also be upgrading a skill set that will serve you well in the new job. Those combined activities will help relieve stress. And you can then take a break and read the paper.

MEDITATION AND MIND CONTROL

"...all that they are capable of becoming."
—Abraham Maslow

———⚬⚬⚬———

Transcendental meditation ™ is a stress reducing technique from the Eastern mystics. It was a training course in the 70's that touted its connection to the Maharishi Mahesh Yogi, which supposedly gave it cachet. For about $125 you were taught how to meditate and what the benefits of such meditation were. Once you learned the mind control and physical control benefits of silencing your mind and contemplating the stark blackness of deep space, you were taught a mantra, a word to repeat over and over again that would help you achieve these benefits. That word was to be kept secret, as it was tailored for your own personality and needs.

I don't want to make fun of the concept, because I believe the benefits are substantial. But in the middle 70's Dr. Herbert Benson wrote a book called *The Relaxation Response,* in which he described how to use the technique and identified its physiological benefits. The book cost $7.95 then.

Both essentially say to relax, close your eyes, and visualize deep space. Dark, silent deep space. Let your mind engage in no conversations with others or itself. Think not about things on-going, just try to think about silent darkness and let the mind go where it will. Take long deep breaths, exhaling slowly. And say the word "One." Over and over. Slowly, calmly.

The process releases endorphins, those glandular secretions that make you feel good. "Runners High" is said to be caused by the release of endorphins. Alcohol is said to restrict the release of endorphins but to substitute itself for them. That's partly why health advisors caution against too much alcohol: it can replace the natural endorphins and without nearly as much health benefit.

I recommend the process and the technique as legitimate. Whenever I feel extreme stress, I find I can fall back on meditation and gain relief. I particularly use it on the airline flights that run into heavy turbulence. In fact, while with the Peace Corps in the early sixties and flying ancient DC-3's around Luzon, I found the technique useful in handling airsickness. And fear. My later training in TM just confirmed what I'd learned earlier. It's useful when I can't sleep for any reason, as well.

I also find it valuable to smile while I exhale. Something about smiling while exhaling seems to gain benefit. Maybe it's the behaviorist in me that I believe if I act happy, I will be happy. And so the smile adds benefit. I envision the endorphins running down my spinal cord, going to the areas of my body where stress affects them: the lower back, the headache, neck and shoulders, and my stomach. You can direct them where you will, it seems to me. At least I feel I can relax my feet, my legs, and up my body, and that helps me sleep. That's useful stress reduction.

VISUALIZATION

"Imagination is more important than knowledge."
—Albert Einstein

Many practitioners of holistic medicine and alternative medicine tout using meditation and visualization as a way of dealing with disease. They suggest visualizing the tumor in the breast, pancreas, or prostate—whereever—being attacked by the antibodies and endorphins and shrunken until they go away. No medical research evidences that such is effective, but there is much anecdotal evidence of success. If it can even make people believe that they've helped themselves by the process, it has some value. Unless someone uses visualization in lieu of other, acknowledged successful treatment, it can't hurt. So, too, you can use it to reduce stress, lower your blood pressure, and create a positive attitude.

BIOFEEDBACK

Dr. Richard Suinn is a former Mayor and a former head of the Psychology Department at Colorado State University. He has made a career study of Biofeedback, and he says, "Biofeedback works." He has used it to help people with migraines, with high blood pressure, and other maladies. He says the process is simple: you train the patient to use their

mind to do something biological that will have an ameliora-
tive impact upon the problem. For example, headaches can be
reduced by having the patient visualize their forehead getting
warm, then getting warm all over. The process, once learned,
then causes the body to dilate the blood vessels for cooling
and that in turn reduces the headache.

Blood pressure is similar. You visualize yourself feeling more relaxed and taking deep breaths, you do relax and
slow down. In the process you lower your blood pressure.

The same techniques can be used by the stressed,
recently terminated employee.

Use whatever you can, and everything you can, to get
you through it and ready for the next step. All are part of the
fallback position you need at your ready call.

EXPRESSIONS

Several cartoonists have prepared charts showing the range
of emotions possible through expressions. It was I'm sure a
great exercise for a cartoonist, trying to draw differences in
expressions to reflect those emotions. Another did similar and
called it "Emotions." They are revealing, both showing the
same number of emotional responses.

Both charts show thirty expressions

Angry	Ashamed	Anxious	Bored	Cautious
Confident	Confused	Depressed	Disgusted	Embarrased
Ecstatic	Enraged	Echausted	Frightened	Frustrated
Guilty	Happy	Hopeful	Hysterical	Jealous
Lonely	Lovestruck	Mischievous	Overwhelmed	Sad
Shocked	Shy	Smug	Surprised	Suspicious

Of those thirty, only five would you consider to be **positive: Ecstatic, Confident, Happy, Hopeful,** and **Lovestruck.** With the possibility of adding **Smug** as a positive.

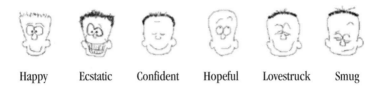

| Happy | Ecstatic | Confident | Hopeful | Lovestruck | Smug |

Isn't it interesting how many more negative emotions we've developed over the eons than we have positive ones? Is it because there is so much more negative that can occur to us than is positive? Or is it merely that we react to the things that occur to us more negatively than positively. Is it because the human mind tends to dwell on the negative more than the positive? Why is that?

Let's look at those emotions, break them down a little further:

A fair number of the emotions seem to be derived from fear: **Suspicion, Embarrassed, Frightened, Cautious, Anxious,** and **Shocked.**

| Suspicion | Embarrassed | Frightened | Cautious | Anxious | Shocked |

Another group derives from the unknown: **Confused, Shy, Suspicious**

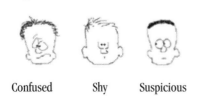

| Confused | Shy | Suspicious |

Others come from letting the emotions get out of control: **Angry, Enraged, Hysterical, Depressed,** and **Frustrated.**

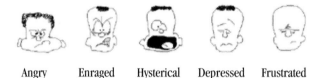

Angry   Enraged   Hysterical   Depressed   Frustrated

Some from not letting the emotions get involved: **Lonely, Shy, Bored.**

Lonely   Shy   Bored

Some come from what you did, acts of commission: **Guilty, Embarrassed, Ashamed.**

Guilty   Embarrassed   Ashamed

Some from acts you may like to take: **Mischievous, Hopeful, Jealous.**

Mischievous   Hopeful   Jealous

Some come from what you didn't do, acts of omission: **Guilty, Ashamed, Frustrated, Overwhelmed, Depressed.**

Guilty   Ashamed   Frustrated   Overwhelmed   Depressed

What can we learn from those?

Five are positive, 25 are negative. Six reflect fear, 3 the unknown, 5 come from the emotions being out of control, 3 the emotions not involved, 3 from acts committed, 3 from acts one would like to take, and 5 from acts that perhaps should have been taken.

There is some overlap in interpretation here too. Some of the emotions are counted in more than just one category.

But it's pretty clear that whether we act or don't act, whether we are uninvolved or involved, make mistakes or are guilty from omissions, we have 5 times more chance of having a negative reaction than a positive one.

There's a lesson there, a kind of a pop psychology lesson, that says whatever you do, you're more likely to be unhappy with it than happy, so whatever you do—including doing nothing, you're going to have to work at being comfortable and pleased with it and with yourself. If that's so with most events, it clearly means you have to work at happiness in the midst of a termination.

KEEP EXERCISING

Today, almost everyone knows the beneficial effects of exercise, even about its stress-reducing qualities. Runners talk about "runner's high," which researchers suggest comes from the release of endorphins from the pituitary. Endorphins create a feeling of euphoria. True, regular exercise makes the body feel good, but it also stimulates the brain toward good feelings.

Alcohol apparently creates a similar feeling to the one produced by endorphins. But researchers suggest that alcohol interferes with the natural production of endorphins.

DON'T FORGET TO PAY ATTENTION TO NUTRITION

> *"When sorrows come,*
> *they come not single spies,*
> *But in battalions."*
> **—King Claudius, Hamlet**

It's awfully easy to fall into a pattern of drinking too much coffee, re-starting smoking, or consuming too much alcohol during these periods of transition. Good nutrition is important at all times, but particularly during periods of stress. Any changed behavior on consumables is cause for reflection and modification. You don't need the additional stress. Consumption is something you can control, while some of the other things happening are not within your control.

CARL SAGAN'S COSMIC CALENDAR

Dr. Sagan, the late renowned scientist and communicator of things obscure, created a calendar to illustrate the time it has taken since the Big Bang to get the cosmos into its present form at this point in time. It is an excellent metaphor for describing the immense amount of time that has elapsed since the Big Bang, estimated to have occurred about 18 billion years ago.

His calendar suggests considering that the Big Bang occurred on January 1. If the 18 billion years were reduced to one year, Sagan suggested, then the year would have played out this way:

- *The gases and debris following the Big Bang expanded at the speed of light for about nine months in all directions.*

- *About the first of May the Milky Way Galaxy formed.*

- *About September 9 the particles congealed and our solar system was formed.*

- *On September 14 the earth was formed.*

- *About September 25, life began on earth.*

- *The first dinosaurs didn't develop until December 24.*

- *The first mammals showed up about December 26.*

- *Dinosaurs were extinct on December 28.*

- *The first humans appeared on December 31, at about 10:30 PM.*

- *The first cities appeared at 11:59:35 p.m.*

- *The Bronze Age began at 11:59:53 PM.*

- *The birth of Christ happened at 11:59:56 PM.*

- *The Renaissance in Europe, the voyages of discovery from Europe, and the experimental method in science all took place at 11:59:59 PM.*

- *The widespread development of science and technology took place at midnight.*

I've often thought of this calendar while sitting in a council meeting with the public, and the public or the council were chewing on my butt. Sagan's calendar shows that the time we are on earth is just a snap of the fingers in the history of time.

While that's somewhat facetious, it helps me to put the comments and conflict in perspective. And it might help you.

REFLECT ON THE GIFTS GAINED FROM THE LAST JOB

Keeping your eye on the positive always lifts the spirits. It will also help put in perspective the fact that you've learned a good deal in the job from which you may be fired. Keep in your WDFWFY (What Do You Want For Yourself) notebook a listing of the key gains you are making on the job. That helps with the resume you need to update annually, but it will also include some skills and abilities that you don't put on the resume. Mistakes would be one example. Bill Ray, in **Walking on Thin Air,** says after a firing take the time to ask the key questions:

- *Out of everything that happened, what skills or attributes served me well over the course of my tenure?*

- *What new skills did I acquire?*

- *What lessons have I learned about project management, public speaking, consensus building, conflict management, goal setting, etc.?*

- *What were the biggest frustrations? What can I do , or what skills will I need, to avoid or minimize that frustration next time around?*

- *If I had it to do over, what would I do over?*

- *What are my biggest weaknesses? What will I do with this time to improve?*

- *What was the most fun? What will I do to replicate it next time around?*

Those questions should not wait for a firing. They should be part of your self-analysis and preparation of your Fallback Position. Learning about yourself is the most important part of the preparation. These are good questions to ask yourself at least yearly.

But also, knowing the answers to those questions is great preparation for the next job interview.

FEELING SORRY FOR YOURSELF

"Fat chance and slim chance mean the same thing."
—Anon.

It's easy now to feel sorry for yourself. But consider other situations. Have some perspective. You have friends who have lost children. Spouses. Accidents, usually car wrecks. Drug overdoses. Important lives cut short by events beyond your control, probably beyond theirs. Disease ravaging bodies slowly, until death mercifully takes them. Families grieving deeply. Your problems are much less severe, much less permanent. You can recover, regroup, and live to fight again. Remember that. It's only the dead that cannot.

Sure, being fired is a lot like the "little death" that Magruder defined. But it's not death. You still have the chance to recover and grow and develop. Think perspective. Take the long view: How can you recover and make the most of the situation? How can you learn from the events? How can you best

158   FALLBACK POSITION

the sumbitch that fired you? Think about the folks in history who suffered severe setbacks and then recovered. Winston Churchill comes to mind as one of the best examples. He was fired as a boy wonder at age 26 as the Minister of the Navy during WWI for the errors at the battle of Gallipoli. Yet he came back, and warned of the threat of Nazi Germany during the late 30's, was hooted by Parliament for years, yet continued his warnings, and then, at age 65 was made Prime Minister when his prophecies proved right. He led the fight for Britain—against advisors who suggested compromise with Hitler—and he was right and made his vision right by his actions. Is there anyone who overcame more adversity you can think of?

Your situation is not worse than his, is it?

Listen to Rabbi Harold Kushner, who wrote **When Bad Things Happen to Good People.** He said this: "Those who cope effectively have a strong sense of self-esteem. When life deals them crushing blows, they tell themselves, 'I can get over this.' Then they do."

You can do it yourself. Don't let yourself get down on yourself.

MAINTAIN PROFESSIONAL CONTACTS

It is well-known that terminations occur, and if it hasn't happened to you, it most likely will. Sometime, somewhere. So while we offer support and understanding to our friends and associates who currently are going through the process, we need to develop a mind-set that shows a willingness to continue those professional contacts when we are going through it.

Most professions have a problem supporting a fellow in-between jobs: "A manager in distress often becomes invisible," is the phrase many use to describe what happens. Then they say, "Don't."

The point these organizations are making is that those fired should not withdraw from the professional contacts and associates with whom they have worked. The manager or employee in such a transition is wanted; he or she should stay in the loop and participate with all associations.

People in such a transition fear that they will not be welcome, that the tenuous nature of every employee's grip on job security is made all too vivid by their presence. Much as a funeral reminds us all that we're mortal. "Ask Not For Whom the Bell Tolls." Or as general aviation pilots say of pilots who fly small planes with retractable landing gear: "There are only two kinds of private pilots who have retractable gear: those who have landed with gear up and those who have yet to do so." The fired employee reminds those who have not been that they have yet to be so.

There's also the fear that those experiencing job loss will be thought less capable than those still employed. Everyone knows that the "Agnes Allen's First Rule of Wing-walking" applies to all positions: "Never let go of what you have a hold of 'til you've got hold of something else." It is easier to get a job from within a job than it is from without. But we all recognize that sometimes job loss is beyond our control.

MAINTAIN PERSONAL CONTACTS WITH FRIENDS AND FAMILY

When in such a transition, we feel a natural reluctance to stay closely in touch with friends and family. Whether rationally or not, we feel that we've let them down. And we feel that they won't understand our profession as well as our associates do.

Like professional police officers, who often believe that only another cop can understand the unique stresses and strains that the job places on the individual and the family, the manager or executive has a similar apprehension: friends and family outside the profession may not understand that the firing may be entirely other than the firee's doing. No error of commission or omission may have been made. The interests of the personalities on the hiring authority may just have been different from the manager's.

Still, we need to continue to be involved with those friends and family members. They may need time in understanding what's going on. But we need to help them and, in so doing, to help ourselves. The explanation process is healing.

∽∾

CHAPTER 7

The Likelihood of You Being Fired In a Career

Never make predictions;
especially about the future:
—Chinese Proverb

———∞∞∞———

DOES THE NAME ENRON OR WORLDCOM OR SUNBEAM MEAN ANYTHING TO YOU?

If there's anything to be learned from the scandals of Enron and WorldCom, it is indisputable that the bosses were not looking out for the employees. They weren't looking out for the shareholders either. Do you recall how many Enron employees were "just sure" that Mr. Ken Lay wouldn't "do anything to hurt them." This while he was urging them to keep their Enron stock in their 401 (k) accounts, as it was plummeting, and he'd already sold. WorldCom was somewhat similar but more akin to a Ponzi scheme, of buying company after company and adding the debt for each purpose to the load, hoping that somewhere down the road the revenue from the whole thing would exceed the revenue from the sum of the parts. Mr. Bernie Ebbers all the while, **Time** magazine reported, was leveraging his company's credit for his personal use, getting the banks to grant him personal loans his collateral didn't cover, the banks betting on the come of a future banking transaction from the company. Then the stock dropped and his collateral was the stock and that forced a margin call, which forced him to sell. The company bailed him out once or twice, to keep the board members' stock from dropping as Ebbers sold. Did they tell the employees to get out or be cautious? Or anything? No. Of course not.

Sunbeam's Al "Chainsaw" Dunlap made a career out of lopping off heads—downsizing, was the euphemism, so investors would think the costs were being cut and the company would be more profitable. What really was happening was he was getting bonuses and options as the value of the stock went up. Who benefited? The board members who had stock. The stockholders, briefly, until the truth was known. The employees? Not on your life.

WILL YOUR CAPTAIN GO DOWN WITH THE SHIP WHILE SAVING YOU?

Do you think your CEO is like the Captain of the ship: He'll be the last off the boat and the last into the lifeboat, making sure all aboard are there first? [Presumably you're smarter than that.]

The world is changing and changing fast. The idea of lifetime employment has been abandoned even by the Japanese, who had the concept imbedded in the culture. As Tom Peters said, "Dramatic change often comes as a response to imminent collapse."

Most professionals don't think they will ever be fired. They are confident, believe they work hard, will be recognized by their hiring authorities, and performance will out. For most of them, that is true. But there are those who hire you who change: they become Dilbert's pointy-haired boss; they become mentally defective because of the stresses their bosses put on them; they make mistakes and then look for scape-goats. The people we hire change over time and we have to watch for those changes to guard against workplace violence. We don't usually expect those changes in our bosses, but they occur. They're not yet considered changes equivalent to work-place violence, but they can have similar consequences. The odds of you not ever working for someone who changes sig-nificantly is infinite to one. Keep your eyes open and your nerve ends sensitive.

I once was followed by a manager who came in with a rep-utation for laying off people. I was writing a newspaper column at the time and he asked if I would please not write about his proposed budget. Since I hadn't seen it, I agreed. Turns out, he said I had left the finances in disarray and he needed to lay people off to balance the budget. A big "to-do" followed, with his finance director saying the budget was out of balance and more, and he laid off a dozen employees. Some sued, three of them for $300,000 in damages. Three years later, the court awarded them $800,000, the difference being punitive damages, because on the witness stand the finance director said there had been no problem with the finances. So whether you're in public or in private, there is reason to be suspicious and cautious about your organization.

HEADLINES AND CLIPPINGS
FROM NEWSPAPERS:

Lucent Lays Off 7,000

HP Cuts 4,000

WorldCom Lays Off 17,000

Intel Cuts 7,000

Sprint Cuts Another 10,000 jobs

J.P.Morgan Cuts 3,000

**Al "Chainsaw" Dunlap cuts 10,000 employees
at Sunbeam.**

Kmart Files for Bankruptcy.

**Enron the Largest Bankruptcy at $60 Billion
in Assets: 2001**

**WorldCom the Largest Bankruptcy at
$103 Billion: 2002**

**American Airlines Asks Employee Unions to
Take Cuts to Avoid Bankruptcy**

American Airlines Execs Fix Pensions for Themselves

**Sun Microsystems CEO Takes $30 Million Salary
While Stock Plummets to $3**

Tyco Exec Takes $20 Million Salary While Indicted

*"Clean Out Your Office in 30 Minutes and Be Off the
Premises or Be Charged with Trespassing."*

CHAPTER 8

Life is Self-Correcting

"Life is an experiment. So plan on making mistakes."
—Source unknown

———∞∞∞———

Termination obviously is not the worst thing that could happen to you. At the moment it makes the other problems seem less onerous. But realistically, it is but a transition. You've been through many worse. Junior High was a transition. Now that was tough.

Death will be a transition. That too will be tough. We think. We know much less than we think we know.

Nothing is to Be Taken Seriously

Life shouldn't be taken seriously.
Approach it as if nothing in life is serious;
As if all its struggles are fun tests of character.
The only serious thing in life is death,
And that's only for those left behind.
The dead are at peace.
Either in Afterlife or in Oblivion—
Unless you believe as some do that you keep coming back
Until you get it right.
In which case perhaps the birth wail is the last evidence
Of the sentient spirit from the other side,
Recognizing it still doesn't get it.

—jea, 2002

*"Look, just because you don't understand it
and I can't explain it,
doesn't mean it's not a good idea."*

—Al Ullman

———

FATE VS. LIFE PLANNING

Many of the exercises in this book are life planning and a good way to get control of yourself and enjoy your life. Fostered by the self-actualization movement, life planning was and is another way of enhancing how you think about yourself. But it is also a means of making your available time most useful and enjoyable.

One exercise I recall was to list all the events in your life that were most important. Key happenings. Clear changes in direction, which maybe you couldn't recognize at the time, but in looking back, you saw clearly as the kinds of forks in the roads that Robert Frost envisioned in his poem, ———

"Two roads diverged in a wood and I,
"I took the one less traveled by.
"And that's made all the difference."

Upon completion of the exercise, you find that almost none of the key events in your life or in almost anyone else's life was planned. The events just happened. You had very little control over them, didn't recognize them as particularly important at the time, and only later did you find them to be seminal.

I went to the Peace Corps, to spend two years in the Philippine Islands because my college roommates chided me for responding to Kennedy's idea of the Peace Corps. I said, "I'd like to do that," and they said in unison, "They wouldn't want you and you couldn't get in."

With that kind of a taunt, I had to try. I took the test the first time it was given, and got a nice letter apparently signed by John F. Kennedy, saying in effect that I was still a Junior in college and I should graduate and then apply to the Peace Corps. I figured you don't ignore career counseling from the President of the United States.

The next year I was asked to go to Hawaii for two months of Peace Corps training. Hawaii. From Kansas to Hawaii. No commitment until the completion of Peace Corps training. Hoo-boy. Pretty heady stuff for a 22-year old.

I got in. But before I went, I worked for three months in my home town of Atchison, Kansas, as an assistant to the city manager. That's another fatalistic story. There I worked with a number of people, including the Manager of the Chamber of Commerce, Claude Odland.

Later, when I was in the Philippines, Claude told my Mom that if I was ever near Manila Air Force Base, to look up CWO Henry Monteiro, who was his cousin from North Dakota, "because he has two daughters and would surely be good for a home-cooked meal."

Well, as soon as I was in Manila, I tried to find the air base. But there isn't any such.

About a year later, I was sent to Clark Air Force Base for dental work. A bridge I had broke and had to be replaced. So they sent me to Clark. While sitting in an air-conditioned, NCO club, having a scotch and water with real ice, watching a movie on television, and thinking what a delightful change this was from my house in Paoay, where there weren't even screens on the windows, and a shower was a coconut shell and a bucket, I thought about Claude. I was doing all right at the moment, maybe I was on a roll. So I went to the phone book and looked up Monteiro. It was there. With a CWO HFT in front.

I hadn't a clue what those initials stood for or how to address the holder. What if he answered the phone and I addressed a "Colonel" as a "Chief"? Blow the home-cooked meal right there. What was a CWO? The Peace Corps training, as extensive as it was, didn't do the table of organization or the protocols of the U.S. Air Force.

So I figured, home-cooked meal, couple of daughters, I'll just have to fake it.

I called the office and asked if "*mumble-mumble* Henry Monteiro was there." The airman answering said, "Sure. Hold on... Mr. Monteiro, it's for you." I thought, "*Mister* Monteiro," that's not too tough. I wonder if he is.

Mr. Monteiro got on the phone and I identified myself and asked if he were a cousin of Claude Odland. He said his wife was and asked very nicely how I knew the North Dakota connection "way over here." I told him the story and he invited me to come to the Officer's Club where he would buy me a drink. I agreed, of course.

He gave me directions and set the time at about 45 minutes from then. I asked how I'd recognize him and he said to go to the reception desk and introduce myself to the lady there, his daughter, Kaye, and he'd meet me. They did invite me to dinner that night, as they did several times; I did have to come back to Clark for more dental work, several times, and I got to know the family. I also learned that CWO meant Chief Warrant Officer and the correct address for a CWO is "Mister." Remember the movie "Mister Roberts".

Kaye and I have been married 38 years now. As much as I believe in the process of life planning, I can't tell how I had any kind of control over that set of events.

PLANS CHANGE

When our son, Jay, went off to college, he wanted to major in Computer Science in the Engineering School. We had bought one of the early micro computers in the late 70's and he had learned to program in Basic and was skilled at it. He was a hard-working student, he learned fast, and did well in most subjects.

When I went to college I majored first in music education, desiring to be a college marching band conductor. I didn't do well enough in the subject to suit me or to persuade me that music was my natural direction. Besides there were too many music courses and not enough of other things. That seemed to me to be putting too many eggs in one basket. So I switched to liberal arts, majoring first in pre-med, then in psychology, and then in personnel administration.

So I advised my son to follow the liberal arts approach, because, I said, "you'll change your mind once or twice as you explore. You don't want to put all your eggs in one basket," I said.

"No, Dad, I want to major in computer science."

Well, that conversation was held several times over about 18 months, all with the same result. You recognize you provide them with the best, you do your best to educate them, but if it doesn't take, it doesn't take. Finally, the parent has to let the kids make their own mistakes.

Jay went off to college with three friends, buddies from the fifth grade, all majoring in computer science.

Three of the four dropped computer science over the next two years. One went to accounting and business the second year, another to journalism the third year, and the third to dance in his fourth year. One stayed with computer science.

Of course Jay was the one staying with computer science. He never varied, loved it all the way through, did really well, and got a good job right upon graduation.

But the exception makes the rule. Three of four had the Fates working on them more than planning.

For our youngest, L.T., who decided he wanted to major in Marine Biology, a degree I suggested was a better graduate program than an undergrad program, "Besides," I said, that was "putting all your eggs in one basket...you'll change your preferences and your major a couple of times, etc. etc. etc. We were living in Colorado so I said, "You ought to go to Colorado University for a couple of years, learn how to go to college, explore different fields, and then decide."

"Forget it," he said. Look what his brother had done, he said: clear direction, unity of purpose, a goal. He was going to do the same thing, be the same way. He was talking sound life planning.

You provide them with the best, you try your best to educate them, but if it doesn't take, it doesn't take. They have to be allowed to make their own mistakes.

For months then, we're looking at schools from Miami to Seattle, agreeing finally on Cal State at Long Beach, ready to write a big check the next day. He comes down in the morning and says, "I think it's a better idea if I go to CU for a year and major in biology in the liberal arts program and take special paramedic training so I have that to fall back on." Smart kid. Plans change.

EVERYONE MAKES MISTAKES

"People who don't take risks
generally make about two big mistakes a year.
People who DO take risks
generally make about two big mistakes a year."
—Peter Drucker

Whenever you are feeling like you've screwed up and you're chewing on yourself, whether that's because you figure someone else will chew on you or because your pride is hurt, you have to get to a mind-set that allows you to recognize that everyone makes mistakes. Then you can forgive yourself. We cannot predict the future, and a great proportion of mistakes become mistakes because of misjudging what is going to happen.

Learn from the past. See if your mis-judgments measure up to some of these great thinkers and policy-makers:

"This telephone has too many shortcomings to be seriously considered as a means of communication. The device is inherently of no value to us."
—Western Union internal memo, 1876

"The wireless music box has no imaginable commercial value. Who would pay for a message sent to nobody in particlular?"

—David Sarnoff's associates in response to his urging for investment in the radio in the 1920's.

"Who the hell wants to hear actors talk?"

—H.M. Warner, Warner Brothers, 1927

"We don't like their sound, and guitar music is on the way out."

—Decca Recording Co. rejecting the Beatles, 1962

"Heavier-than-air flying machines are impossible."

—Lord Kelvin, President, Royal Society, 1895

"I think there's a world market for about five computers."

—Thomas J. Watson, Chairman of the Board, IBM

"The bomb will never go off. I speak as an expert in explosives."

—Admiral William Leahy, US Atomic Bomb Project

"Stocks have reached what looks like a permanently high plateau."

—Irving Fisher, Professor of Economics, Yale University, 1929

"Airplanes are interesting toys but of no military value."

—Marchal Foch, Professor of Strategy, Ecole Superieure de Guerre

*"Man will never reach the moon regardless
of all scientific advances."*

**—Dr. Lee De Forest, inventor of the vacuum tube
and father of television.**

"Everything that can be invented has been invented."

**—Charles H. Duell, Commissioner,
U.S. Office of Patents, 1899**

— These comments were downloaded from the Internet with no
source attributed to them. So whoever assembled the collec-
tion, I'm indebted to you. They are wonderful examples of the
recent thought of British Prime Minister Tony Blair: "I never
make predictions about the future. Never have. Never will."

COMPROMISE, TOO

"The better part of valor is discretion"

—Falstaff, Henry IV

Besides not worrying too much about mistakes, the other
side of the coin is that even if you think you know the answer,
sometimes you cannot convince your employer that it is correct. They want to go another direction and you, having
worked on the decision, have thought about that option,
rejected it, and believe your recommendation is more sound.

My first mentor, Al Thelen, suggested you have to compromise if you are going to be successful. You shouldn't be in a
key position if you can't compromise. Besides, you don't
know everything; your judgment is not infallible.

If that's not enough rationale for you, remember the military advice, "To get ahead, go along."

Wherever you work, there is still someone whose judgment

organizationally is superior to yours. As they say, "The boss is not always right, but he is always the boss." Be prepared to compromise.

Now this advice doesn't work for questions of legality or morality. You need to stick to your guns when it comes to keeping the boss and yourself from going to jail. It's a fairly expected but unspoken part of your role.

If compromise is difficult for you, it doesn't have to be that visible. Most of the people observing cannot read your mind, and if you duck your head on one issue, no one needs to know. So you can live to fight another battle. It's not courageous to allow your head to be taken off. If someone swings an axe, it's okay to duck.

There are a few absolutes about compromise, in my judgment. These fall into the category of abuse of privilege or abuse of power.

- ***Don't give money away.*** *Always get fair value in return. It's part of the stewardship role that you sign on for as an executive. It's a trust role that goes with the territory. It's also essential for your credibility.*

- ***Don't reward friends or punish enemies just for the sake of reward or punishment.*** *Make decisions based on your best judgment of what's good for the organization you serve.*

- ***Don't use the power or wealth of the organization for political purposes.*** *I've seen city councils sue contractors and admit the suit was "for political purposes."*

GREAT EXPERIENCES: THE FLOODS

"I know of no higher fortitude than stubbornness in the face of overwhelming odds."
—Louis Nizer

My first city manager job was in Minot, North Dakota. A city of 35,000 hard-working, good natured people. It had a city council of fourteen people, a directly-elected Mayor with a veto, and an employee complement of 315. My first day there they had a reception for me and the Chair of the Planning Commission pinned a big red button me that said, "-44 Degrees Keeps Out the Riff-Raff." They made an exception for me, I guess, and three months later when it was 42 degrees below zero and the wind was howling to a 96 degrees below zero wind chill factor, I wondered about my decision.

Later, I went to an economic development meeting and they were considering a new promotional slogan. I asked what the old one was. They said, "Why Not, Minot?"

Six months later the U.S. Weather Service called and told me we had a flood coming down from snow melt in Canada. It would exceed the river's flowing capacity by about two feet. We had to build dikes to contain it, along fifteen miles of residence-lined river bank through town. The City Council passed a resolution putting all authority for accomplishment on me, as City Manager. We had three weeks. It was a big job but the city staff got it done.

Two years later the same thing happened. We successfully increased the size of the dikes again. Hard work, but successful.

Then in my fifth year there, my now friends at the Weather Service called and said "We've got real trouble. Right here in River City." They've measured the snow depth in Canada, they said, and "within three weeks you will have water running in the river, at a flow rate that would be ten feet deeper than the channel can carry, if you could keep it in the channel."

The City Council passed two Resolutions: one asking the U.S. Corps of Engineers to come in and help build the dikes. That provided that the City would acquire the needed right of way. The other Resolution put all authority in the City Manager to condemn right of way, confiscate private property, tear it down, relocate it, coordinate the Corps of Engineers contractors, and essentially do whatever was necessary to get the dikes built ten feet higher than the surrounding grade. As the Resolution was being read, and it became more and more clear that the responsibility for success or failure was being put on my shoulders—in a way that would brook no confusion about accountability—the City Attorney who had drafted the Resolution, leaned over and whispered in my ear, "Hitler came to power with less authority."

The Corps came in under the leadership of a Colonel, Max Noah. I'm fighting a flood with a guy named Noah! I thought, Is that good or bad?

At one point Colonel Noah called me on the phone. We had a problem with a landowner who wouldn't let the Corps contractors on his land. I went to the site where dozers and dump trucks were lined up and ready to go, and Colonel Noah was anxious to give the order. I listened to the landowner and then explained to him that we had to go in his backyard and build the dikes. He was at a critical, outside curve with a lot of pressure and erosion coming. He complained again that it would destroy his barbecue and his backyard landscaping and he didn't want it there. I had to tell him we had to move quickly to build the dike and he could either have it on the river side of his house or around the front of his house, curving back to the river. He said, "But that would put my house in the flood!" I nodded and agreed he had the proper understanding of the situation. "You would do that?" he asked, incredulously. "Yes," I told him. "I have no choice." He agreed to let us build the dike in his backyard. The dozers and trucks moved immediately.

Another time the Governor was coming to town to inspect our efforts and see what he could do to help. By then the dikes were up and the flood waters were rushing through town, as predicted ten feet above the grade. We took a city bus and the Mayor and Governor to a railroad trestle that was under water crossing the river, with a dike perpendicular to the tracks on top. The Mayor and Governor climbed the dike and looked at the raging water. As I stood below the dike, I could see the dike was leaking right beneath where they were standing. Because this was a curve, the pressure to erode was great. I had the thought that the dike could go anytime, but I was consoled that if it went and got the Mayor and Governor, it would also get me, and no one would know I knew the dike was leaking. I immediately called for emergency patching. Our crews were there to shore it up before the Mayor and Governor got off the dike. It was with some relief that both occurred without incident.

We then went to a press conference and the Corps called me on the way, saying another site on the western edge of town was eroding badly and they needed new clay to plug the hole for compaction. The only site that had the material close by was an under-construction highway interchange that the state was building. I told them to go get the material and I'd ask the Governor for permission.

I got off the radio just as we walked into the Council Chambers for the Press Conference and went to the Governor's side and whispered, "Governor, I need to ask you for permission to use some of the clay on the highway inter-change for an emergency fix. We'll replace it later. I sure hope you say yes because I've already authorized our guys to go get the clay."

He just looked at me, blinked a couple of times, and nod-ded. We went through the public request and he said the "state would be pleased to help."

Good people.

At one point the Corps determined we needed a cut made through a park, to reduce the constriction on flow. The park had been constructed with a federal grant some years before. But any change to federally funded parks needed the signa-ture of the Secretary of the Interior. That usually took about 18 months of review. Our Congressional Delegation was made aware and went to work. We got the approval in four days.

Another cut was needed through an occupied location. I assigned the Urban Renewal Director and the Director of Finance to go purchase the property and get the building relo-cated—by the next morning! They walked into the auto repair shop, with the owner on a crawler under a truck, and said, "We want to buy your building. How much do you want for it?"

He said, "It's not for sale."

They said, "We're buying it and that's final."

He then crawled out from under it and asked, "You and whose army?"

They knew the owner and so said, "The U.S. Army."

They explained the situation, negotiated a price, including relocating his metal building, and the building was gone, and the Corps contractors dug that cut the next morning.

After two weeks of rushing water and patching and creating secondary dikes, and in some places tertiary dikes, the Corps came to me on a Sunday night, after it had been raining, saying "We're afraid the dikes are going to fail. We need to evacuate."

Well, there were 12,000 people and 4,200 homes at risk. A broken dike is ten foot deep water going fast. Hundreds if not thousands of lives were at risk.

We had prepared for that eventuality, with trucks and buses, and volunteers, and the Air Force Base support.

So we got on television at 8 pm and called a Mandatory Evacuation by midnight. Everyone worked together and we got it done. People stayed out of their homes for about a week. Saying it fast like that makes it sound easy.

I told you, North Dakotans are good, hard-working people.

We held the dikes together and nobody got wet. The Corps did a wonderful job. The City staff did a wonderful job. The community was superbly cooperative.

Later, there was some criticism of my decision about the evacuation because the dikes did not fail. Besides being something of a reminder that no good deed goes unpunished, it was a small consequence.

The point is that wherever you work, in whatever job you

have, there is opportunity to do something worthwhile, to make a contribution to society. To act with decisiveness, to support others, to help build co-workers, to build the organization, is a process that will build you. Not everyone gets the high-risk/high-reward opportunity to lead the fighting of a flood. But as one of my favorite office assistants, who always had a smile, no matter what happened, said, "Bloom where you're planted."

BULLETS I DODGED: JOBS I DIDN'T GET

"Be careful what you wish for,
you just may get it."
—Mothers for generations

As we transition in our lives, we need to remember that things usually work out for the best. I've asked Department Heads to leave, honestly telling them I think the organization had passed them by, or their time had come and gone, years later they've returned to me and said it was one of the best things that ever happened to them, painful as it was at the time.

I think it's important to handle such transitions as humanely as is possible, but the least humane thing to do is to allow the relationship to continue unabated. After trying to retrain, acculturize, re-prioritize, coach, and motivate and failing at it, it is often necessary to make a separation.

At the same time, most of us have encountered the job that looked attractive, that we did not have offered, and that later we discovered was not as it appeared. I've had several.

City Manager of Xenia

The first I can recall was when I was attempting to become a city manager for the first time. I interviewed in Xenia, Ohio—a pretty little town with a Town Square, and a picturesque old brick city hall on the square. I was at the time the Assistant City Manager in Little Rock. (I was looking outside the state as I didn't think there was any political future coming out of Arkansas.) The job was not offered me in Xenia. Later that year I was offered and accepted my first CM job in Minot, North Dakota. Xenia was hit by a tornado the following spring, at the exact time when I was flying to the annual conference of city managers in Kansas. I would have been gone while my wife and two sons were in Xenia.

As Fats Waller said, "One never knows, do one?"

Director of Public Works of Denver

I interviewed with the City of Denver for newly-elected Mayor Wellington Webb's Transition Team, to be Director of Public Works. I had been much involved in public works construction, including in the metro Denver area directing a 50-mile beltway project. I prided myself that I had directed over 125 major public works projects, all coming in on time and within budget. (Before that I had two come in at $50,000 over budget and was embarrassed by a project manager keeping two sets of books—talk about people who needed to move on!) I knew the new Denver International Airport was under construction—and frankly knew it was troubled from what I heard on my road project, which used many of the same engineering and construction firms. The Transition Team nominated me as their first choice, but I apparently didn't hit it off with the Mayor and so was not offered the job. (He actually told friends he thought I was more a "PR Man" than what he wanted.)

That new airport came in two years late and nearly 2.5 Billion dollars over budget. ***Billion!*** *Originally budgeted at $1.8 billion, it came in at $5.3 billion.* I don't know how it's possible to over-run a project by that amount unintentionally.

Talk about dodging a bullet. I know the key thing with construction projects is that those started badly are almost impossible to turn around to end well. I would have been fired for blowing the whistle, or for insubordination over not spending that much more than was authorized, or would have had to be the apologist while it was going on. I wouldn't have been able to do the latter. They really needed a P.R. man.

Chicago Commissioner of Transportation

The then new Mayor Richard Daley had asked a major national headhunter located in Chicago to find a Commissioner of Transportation. Daley was splitting his public works department in two, with the maintenance activities being retained by the old department and a new Commissioner of Transportation to be in charge of construction. Apparently the old line engineers had created a new bridge flyover on a freeway, and on the lake side erected a jersey curb railing so no one could see the lake. A tragic mistake of esthetics, brought about by engineers who didn't want the driving public to be distracted by a view. When the recruiter approached me about being Commissioner and described building light rail and rebuilding all 65 of the beautiful cantilevered bridges crossing the river in the loop, I had to say the new job that involved just the construction was the fun stuff and I'd be very interested.

I was interviewed by the headhunter and they were convinced I had the stuff to do the job well. So they scheduled me first to meet with the Mayor's Chief of Staff. I went and the day I arrived the newspapers had the headline "Budget Deficit Forces Mayor to Lay Off 1500." I told the Chief of Staff that Chicago was a patronage town and they couldn't bring a guy in from Colorado and pay him $150,000 while laying folks off.

I was right, of course. The Mayor promoted an engineer from within and a year later one of the contractors driving pile for one of the bridges punctured the utility tunnel that was below river level and carried all the electronics and the other utilities serving the Loop. It flooded the tunnel and shut down the Loop for a week, causing an estimated $2 billion in damage to business. The engineer in charge said the city's bureaucratic procedures wouldn't allow him to fix the flooding in time.

I told the Chief of Staff that my background in fighting floods and building projects to avoid problems would have led me to solve the problem and I might have gotten fired for violating procedures, but it wouldn't have flooded. Is that ego talking? I don't think so. I think it's common sense to know what's most important and to do what's necessary to protect the public. The procedures are there to protect the public too, but there are times to set them aside. That was one.

IT REALLY IS THE PEOPLE

"Man is the only animal that laughs.
He's also the only animal that has a legislature."
—Betty Ann Dittemore

One year I ran into my good friend, Al Thelen, in the airport on the way to a conference. He and I hadn't seen each other in a year or so, he being out in Montana managing first Helena and then Billings, both under some considerable duress, and both successfully, while I was managing in North Dakota.

We were both flying to a manager's conference and we had some time to visit, time we hadn't had together in many years.

He said, "You know, I've had a couple of my close friends die on me recently, and I've had reason to think about relationships."

I looked closely at him, knowing he was not one to be open about his innermost feelings and realized he was confiding some important thoughts.

He said, "As you go through this life, no matter how successful you are or think you are, no matter the rewards or honors, it really is the people you meet along the way, isn't it?"

I agreed. And then as he talked a little about the friends he'd lost, I recalled our relationship.

He was the one person most responsible for starting me in a career in city management and encouraging me. He hired me as intern in his first city management job. He was 27 and I was 22. He had begun his first city management job in my home town of Atchison, Kansas, about six months before.

My undergraduate degree in personnel administration required a six-week "internship," a real-world working experience in a personnel office dealing with and solving the problems facing people working in organizations. Most of the interns worked in business, but a few worked in mental hospitals and other public agencies.

To go back to my own experience, I hadn't much cared

where I went to college because my degree was just an expedient: I had majored in music education and psychology, changing yearly as the courses I took suited my fancy and as thoughts of future careers seemed fitting. Music education required too much commitment to one area; almost all but a few core courses were music. That seemed to fit the cliché of "putting all your eggs in one basket," and unless you were superbly skilled, which I quickly noticed in comparison to the others I was not, it seemed an unwise option.

Psychology was fascinating and the opportunity to take all the other interesting courses in the liberal arts curriculum was attractive. Then too, the degree led to the possibility of going on into medicine and perhaps being a psychiatrist—something I could perhaps use to help my dad, which had significant motivational appeal.

But the idea of going to school for at least seven years for a medical degree and then a couple of more years for the specialty didn't seem appropriate for my financial backing, or for my level of interest in school.

The deciding point was when I took zoology and found in dissecting a guinea pig that the veins and arteries and nerves all were different shades of red and pink and green and my red/green color blindness made successful surgery more than just problematic.

So I was looking through the course catalogue in my junior year, wondering how I could get out of this chicken outfit with what constituted an honorable discharge, when I found the degree in Personnel Administration. A chance for a sheepskin without tossing out everything I'd taken.

It required a few courses I hadn't taken, but many more

that I had. A natural.

My advisor in Personnel Administration was Dr. William Cape. A fine man, a scholar, a researcher, and acting head of the department, along with acting head of the public administration master's degree program. Also a South Dakota native. He was a friend of Al Thelen.

He said. "You need an internship and Al is the new city manager of Atchison, your home town."

So far so good, I thought. What's a city manager?

He said, "Al needs an intern to go in and set up a personnel system—from scratch. He's new and it's his first job and he's asked if I can give him an intern."

Good, I thought. What's a city manager?

He went on, "You could live at home for no cost, (the interns weren't paid) and fulfill your requirements for a degree. Would you like to talk to him?"

"Good," I said, quickly. "I'd like to talk to him."

I met with Al, and he said he'd like me to set up a personnel system. That while the city was small, with only 75 employees, it needed a professional personnel system and what they had was not that. He wanted me to begin as soon as I could. Was I interested?"

I said I was.

Then Al surprised me and said, "I want to pay you, even though I know personnel interns are not usually paid."

Well, naturally he had my full attention.

He said, "I want to pay you so I can give you other things besides personnel to do."

"Fine," I said.

"I want you to help me with the budget and with citizen

requests and with weed control procedures," he said.

"Fine," I said, while I thought, What are weed control procedures?

He said, "I'll start you at $30 a week."

"Fine", I said, "That sounds good," noting that was just what I was getting weekly from playing three nights a week in a country-rock band, and I'd been doing it for two years and getting by. His $30 was gravy.

He then had me handle the complaints from little old ladies who had problems with the city's garbage pickup, or little old ladies whose neighbors' cottonwood trees shed in their yards, or little old ladies whose streets needed grading.

I'd go out and visit with them, listen to what the problem was, usually over cookies and milk, talk to the city foreman who was in charge of that area, and try to negotiate a solution that fit the citizen's desire with the city ordinances and policy.

Al also used me to help work through the city budget with all the departments, learning about sewage plants and fire departments and other minutiae of city government. He also took me to meetings with the municipal league and the legislature, exposing me to the big issues of the day.

In between I assembled a reasonable personnel system for a city of that size. Using my high school art teacher for illustrations, I built a personnel manual, that, Al said, was as good as he'd seen.

After six weeks of that he said, "You're doing very well. You understand city government's role so well, I want you to stay on for another month or so and I'll double your salary. $60 a week for the next two months."

Now even in 1962, $60 a week was no great shakes. But

being thought well-enough of to get your salary doubled after six weeks on the job was a heady experience.

Al knew I was going to the Peace Corps sometime in the next few months, so the timing worked fine. I had since learned a bit about what being a city manager was and it was appealing.

Then he popped a real surprise. "I'm going on vacation for two weeks," he said, "and I'd like you to be acting city manager while I'm gone."

Now he got me. "Two months ago," I said, "I didn't even know what a city manager was, and now you want me to be one."

He said, "You can handle it, and it will be good experience for you."

I didn't doubt it. What I didn't know was that it would hook me on local government management.

And Al was right about the people I've met along the way: they really are what it is all about.

On speaking: first have something to say,
second say it,
third stop when you have said it,
and finally give it an accurate title.
—John Shaw Billings

"I hope I've done that."
—JEA, 2003

Appendix A

SUGGESTED FURTHER READINGS

Bolles, Richard Nelson, **The 1995 What Color is Your Parachute?,** Ten Speed Press, Berkeley, CA.

Metcalf, C.W. and Felible, Roma, **Lighten Up**, Survival Skills for People Under Pressure; Addison-Wesley, 1992.

Benson, Herbert, with Klipper, Miriam Z., **The Relaxation Response;** William Morrow; 1976.

Moyers, Bill, **Healing and the Mind**, Doubleday, 1993.

Peck, M. Scott**, The Road Less Traveled,** Simon and Shuster, 1978

Kushner, Harold S., **When Bad Things Happen to Good People,** Avon; 1981

Greene, James, and Lewis, David, **Know Your Own Mind**, Rawson Associates, 1983

Hughes, Richard, **Put Your Best Foot Forward**,

Carver, John**, Boards That Make a Difference**, Jossey-Bass, San Francisco, 1990

Charland, William**, Career Shifting**, Center for the New West, Bob Adams, Inc. 1993

Rubin, Bonnie Miller, **Time Out**, W.W. Norton, New York, 1987.

Covey, Stephen R., **Principle-Centered Leadership**, Simon and Shuster, New York, 1990

Covey, Stephen R., **The 7 Habits of Highly Effective People**, Simon and Shuster, New York, 1989

Cleveland, Harlan, **The Knowledge Executive**, Truman Talley Books, New York, 1985

DePree, Max, **Leadership is an Art**, Dell, New York, 1989

Bennis, Warren, **Why Leaders Can't Lead**, Jossey-Bass, San Francisco, 1989

Galos, Jodie-Beth and McIntosh, Sandy, Ph.D., **Firing Back, Power Strategies for Cutting the Best Deal When You Are About to Lose Your Job**, John Wiley, New York, 1997

Mantell, Michael, **Ticking Bombs, Defusing Violence in the Workplace,** Irwin Publishing, New York, NY, 1994

Pell, Dr. Arthur R., **Complete Idiot's Guide to Managing People,** Alpha Books, New York, NY, 1995

Delpo, Amy and Lisa Guerin, Lisa, Attorneys, **Dealing with Problem Employees,** a Legal Guide, NOLO, Bertelsman Services, Berkeley, CA 2001

Drucker, Peter F., **Managing for the Future,** Truman Talley Books, New York, 1992.

Grote and Harvey, **Discipline Without Punishment.**

Appendix B

SAMPLE EMPLOYMENT AGREEMENT

THIS AGREEMENT, made and entered into this _____ day of _____, 20 ___ by and between the [employer] _____, a corporation, hereinafter called "Employer," as party of the first part, and _____ [name], as party of the second part, both of whom understand as follows:

WITNESSETH:

WHEREAS, Employer desires to employ the services of said _____ [name] as _____ of _____; and

WHEREAS, it is the desire of the Employer to provide certain benefits, to establish certain conditions of employment, and to set working conditions of said Employee; and

WHEREAS, Employee desires to accept employment as _____ of said Employer; and

NOW THEREFORE, in consideration of the mutual covenants herein contained, the parties agree as follows:

SECTION 1: DUTIES

Employer hereby agrees to employ said _____ [name] as _____ of said Employer to perform the functions and duties specified in said job description of the Employer and to perform other legally permissible and proper duties and functions as the Employer shall from time to time assign.

SECTION 2: TERM

A. Employee agrees to remain in the exclusive employ of Employer until _____, 20 ____, and neither to accept other employment nor to become employed by any other employer until said termination date, unless said termination date is affected as hereinafter provided.

B. In the event written notice is not given by either party to this agreement to the other _____ [minimum of 90 days is recommended] prior to the termination date as hereinabove provided, this agreement shall be extended on the same terms and conditions as herein provided, all for an additional period of two years. Said agreement shall continue thereafter for two-year periods unless either party hereto gives _____ days [minimum of 90 days is recommended] written notice to the other party that the party does not wish to extend this agreement for an additional two-year term.

C. Nothing in this agreement shall prevent, limit or otherwise interfere with the right of the Employer to terminate the services of Employee at any time, subject only to the provisions set forth in Section 4, paragraphs A and B, of this agreement.

D. Nothing in this agreement shall prevent, limit or otherwise interfere with the right of the Employee to resign at any time from his position with Employer, subject only to the provision set forth in Section 5 of this agreement.

SECTION 3: SUSPENSION

Employer may suspend the Employee with full pay and benefits at any time during the term of this agreement, but only for cause.

SECTION 4:
TERMINATION AND SEVERANCE PAY

A. In the event Employee is terminated by the Employer before expiration of the aforesaid term of employment and during such time that Employee is willing and able to perform his/her duties under this agreement, then in that event Employer agrees to pay Employee a lump sum cash payment equal to ____ months' aggregate salary, benefits, and deferred compensation. Employee shall also be compensated for all earned sick leave, vacation, holidays, compensatory time, and other accrued benefits to date. In the event Employee is terminated for cause or for conviction, Employer shall have no obligation to pay the aggregate severance sum designated in the above paragraph.

B. In the event Employer at any time during the term of this agreement reduces the salary or other financial benefits of Employee in a greater percentage than an applicable across-the-board reduction for all employees of Employer, or in the event Employer refuses, following written notice, to comply with any other provision benefiting Employee herein, or the Employee resigns following a suggestion, whether formal or informal, by the Employer that he/she resign, then, in that event Employee may, at his/her option, be deemed to be "terminated" at the date of such reduction or such refusal to comply within the meaning and context of the herein severance pay provision.

C. If Employee is terminated, Employer agrees to provide for outplacement services to Employee at its expense, should Employee desire them, in an amount not to exceed a total of $5,000.

SECTION 5: RESIGNATION

In the event Employee voluntarily resigns his/her position

with Employer before expiration of the aforesaid term of his/her employment, then Employee shall give Employer thirty days notice in advance, unless the parties agree otherwise.

SECTION 6: DISABILITY

If Employee is permanently disabled or is otherwise unable to perform his/her duties without reasonable accommodation because of sickness, accident, injury, mental incapacity or health for a period of four successive weeks beyond any accrued sick leave, Employer shall have the option to terminate this agreement, subject to the severance pay requirements of Section 4, paragraph A.

SECTION 7: SALARY

Employer agrees to pay Employee for his/her services rendered pursuant hereto an annual base salary of $_____, payable in installments at the same time as other management employees of the Employer are paid. In addition, Employer agrees to increase said base salary and/or benefits of Employee in such amounts and to such extent as the Employer may determine that it is desirable to do so on the basis of an annual salary review of said Employee made at the same time as similar consideration is given other employees generally.

SECTION 8: PERFORMANCE EVALUATION

A. The Employer shall review and evaluate the performance of the Employee at least once annually in advance of the adoption of the annual operating budget. Said review and evaluation shall be in accordance with specific criteria developed jointly by Employer and Employee. Said criteria may be added to or deleted from as the Employer may from time to time determine, in consultation with the

Employee. Further, the _____(Employer's representative as Employee's supervisor) shall provide the Employee with a summary written statement of the findings of the supervisor and provide an adequate opportunity for the Employee to discuss his/her evaluation with the supervisor or other representative of the Employer.

SECTION 9: HOURS OF WORK

It is recognized that Employee must devote a great deal of time outside the normal office hours to business of the Employer, and to that end Employee will be allowed to take compensatory time off as he/she shall deem appropriate during said normal office hours.

SECTION 10: OUTSIDE ACTIVITIES

Employee shall not spend more than 10 hours per week in teaching, consulting, volunteering or other non-Employer-connected business without the prior approval of the Employer.

SECTION 11: MOVING AND RELOCATION EXPENSES

Employee shall be reimbursed, or Employer may pay directly, for the expenses of packing and moving Employee, Employee's family, and Employee's personal property from _____ to _____ with said payment or reimbursement not to exceed the sum of $_____, which shall include unpacking, any storage costs necessary, and insurance charges.

SECTION 12: HOME SALE AND PURCHASE EXPENSES

A. Employee shall be reimbursed for the direct costs associated with the sale of his/her existing personal residence, said reimbursement being limited to real estate agents' fees, and other closing costs that are directly associated with the sale of the house. Said reimbursement should not exceed the sum of $_____.

B. Employee shall also be reimbursed for the costs incidental to buying a house, including legal services, title insurance, and other costs directly associated with the purchase of the house, said reimbursement not to exceed the sum of $_____.

C. Employer shall provide Employee with a _____ [fixed-interest, variable-interest, interest-only] loan to purchase a house. The amount of the loan shall not exceed $_____.

D. Employer shall provide for temporary housing for Employee, including house-hunting trips as additional compensation, not to exceed $_____.

SECTION 13: AUTOMOBILE

Employee's duties require that he/she shall have the exclusive and unrestricted use at all times during his/her employment with Employer of an automobile provided to him/her by the Employer. Employer shall be responsible for paying for liability, property damage, and comprehensive insurance, and for the purchase, operation, maintenance, repair, and regular replacement of said automobile.

SECTION 14:
VACATION, SICK, AND MILITARY LEAVE

A. As an inducement to Employee to become _____ [job title], at signature hereof, Employee shall be credited with ____ days [number of days granted other employees in one year is recommended] of vacation leave and _____ days [number of days granted other employees in one year is recommended] of sick leave. Thereafter, Employee shall accrue, and have credited to his/her personal account, vacation and sick leave at the same rate as other general employees of Employer.

B. Employee shall be entitled to military reserve leave time pursuant to state law.

SECTION 15:
DISABILITY, HEALTH, AND LIFE INSURANCE

A. Employer agrees to put into force and to make required premium payments for Employee for insurance policies for life, accident, sickness, disability income benefits, major medical, and dependent's coverage group insurance covering Employee and his dependents.

B. Employer agrees to purchase and to pay the required premiums on whole life insurance policies equal in amount to _____ times the annual gross salary of Employee, with the beneficiary named by Employee to receive one-half of any benefits paid, Employer the other one-half.

C. Employer agrees to provide hospitalization, surgical and comprehensive medical insurance for Employee and his dependents and to pay the premiums thereon equal to that which is provided all other employees of Employer or, in the event no such plan exists, to provide same for Employee.

D. Employer shall provide travel insurance for Employee while he/she is traveling on Employer's business, with Employee to name beneficiary thereof.

E. Employee agrees to submit once per calendar year to a complete physical examination by a qualified physician selected by the Employer, the cost of which shall be paid by the Employer.

SECTION 16: RETIREMENT

Employer agrees that in addition to the base salary paid by the Employer to Employee, Employer agrees to pay an amount equal to ____ percent of Employee's base salary into the company 401-k on Employee's behalf, in equal proportionate amounts each pay period, and to transfer ownership to succeeding employers upon Employee's resignation or termination. The parties shall fully disclose to each other the financial impact of any amendment to the terms of Employee's retirement benefit.

SECTION 17: DUES AND SUBSCRIPTIONS

Employer agrees to budget for and to pay for professional dues and subscriptions of Employee necessary for his/her continuation and full participation in national, regional, state, and local associations and organizations necessary and desirable for his/her continued professional participation, growth, and advancement, and for the good of the Employer.

SECTION 18: PROFESSIONAL DEVELOPMENT

A. Employer hereby agrees to budget for and to pay for travel and subsistence expenses of Employee for professional and official travel, meetings, and occasions adequate to continue the professional development of Employee and to adequately pursue necessary official functions for Employer.

B. Employer also agrees to budget for and to pay for travel and subsistence expenses of Employee for short courses, institutes, and seminars that are necessary for his/her professional development and for the good of the Employer.

SECTION 19:
PERSONAL COMPUTER PURCHASE

Employer hereby agrees to purchase a personal computer and software at a cost not to exceed $_____. The Employer provides the money for the total cost and the Employee reimburses the amount in excess of $_____ over a one-year period. Employee must work for the Employer for one full year to qualify for the $_____ subsidy.

SECTION 20: GENERAL EXPENSES

Employer recognizes that certain expenses of a non-personal and generally job-affiliated nature are incurred by Employee, and hereby agrees to reimburse or to pay said general expenses, up to an amount not to exceed $_____ per month, and the finance director is hereby authorized to disburse such moneys upon receipt of duly executed expense or petty cash vouchers, receipts, statements or personal affidavits.

SECTION 21: CIVIC CLUB MEMBERSHIP

Employer recognizes the desirability of representation in and before local civic and other organizations, and Employee is authorized to become a member of _____ such civic clubs or organizations, for which Employer shall pay all expenses. Employee shall report to the Employer on each membership that he has taken out at Employer's expense.

SECTION 22: INDEMNIFICATION

Employer shall defend, save harmless, and indemnify

Employee against any tort, professional liability claim or demand or other legal action, whether groundless or otherwise, arising out of an alleged act or omission occurring in the performance of Employee's duties as [job title]. Employer will compromise and settle any such claim or suit and pay the amount of any settlement or judgment rendered thereon.

SECTION 23: BONDING

Employer shall bear the full cost of any fidelity or other bonds required of the Employee.

SECTION 24: OTHER TERMS AND CONDITIONS OF EMPLOYMENT

A. The Employer, in consultation with the Employee, shall fix any such other terms and conditions of employment, as it may determine from time to time, relating to the performance of Employee, provided such terms and conditions are not inconsistent with or in conflict with the provisions of this agreement or any law.

B. All provisions of the Employer's regulations and rules relating to vacation and sick leave, retirement and pension system contributions, holidays, and other benefits and working conditions as they now exist or hereafter may be amended, also shall apply to Employee as they would to other employees of Employer, in addition to said benefits enumerated specifically for the benefit of Employee except as herein provided.

C. Employee shall be entitled to receive the same vacation and sick leave benefits as are accorded department heads, including provisions governing accrual and payment therefor on termination of employment.

SECTION 25: NO REDUCTION OF BENEFITS

Employer shall not any time during the term of this agreement reduce the salary, compensation or other financial benefits of Employee, except to the degree of such a reduction across-the-board for all employees of the Employer.

SECTION 26:
REPRESENTATION OF EMPLOYER

Employer represents that it has the legal authority to enter into and be bound by the terms of this agreement.

SECTION 27: SEVERABILITY

Should any provision of this agreement be held unlawful by a court of competent jurisdiction, all other provisions of the agreement shall remain in force for the duration of the agreement.

SECTION 28: NOTICES

Notices pursuant to this agreement shall be given by deposit in the custody of the United States Postal Service, postage pre-paid, addressed as follows:

(1)   EMPLOYER:
(2)   EMPLOYEE: [Name and address of Employee]

Alternatively, notices required pursuant to this agreement may be personally served in the same manner as is applicable to civil judicial practice. Notice shall be deemed given as of the date of personal service or as of the date of deposit of such written notice in the course of transmission in the United States Postal Service.

SECTION 29: GENERAL PROVISIONS

A. The text herein shall constitute the entire agreement between the parties.

B. This agreement shall be binding upon and inure to the benefit of the heirs at law and executors of Employee.

C. This agreement shall become effective commencing _____, 20 ____.

D. If any provision, or any portion thereof, contained in this agreement is held unconstitutional, invalid or unenforceable, the remainder of this agreement, or portion thereof, shall be deemed severable, shall not be affected, and shall remain in full force and effect.

IN WITNESS WHEREOF, the Employer of _____ has caused this agreement to be signed and executed in its behalf by its [chief executive officer], and duly attested by its clerk, and the Employee has signed and executed this agreement, both in duplicate, the day and year first above written.

_____

chief executive officer of

_____

_____

Employee

Appendix C

SAMPLE TERMINATION AGREEMENT

Comco and John Sample,
former Marketing Director

This Agreement is made and entered into the 25 th day of April, 2003 by and between John Sample (individual, address), and the Comco (organization), a private company, organized under the laws of Delaware.

FACTUAL RECITALS

John Sample has served as Marketing Director (position) for the Comco under an employment agreement dated _____ .

On April 15, 2003 John Sample tendered, and the CEO of Comco accepted, Sample's resignation as a Marketing Ditector for Comco. Comco and Sample desire to establish the terms by which Sample shall serve as Executive Consultant to Comco through May 31, 2003.

Comco and Sample mutually desire to agree to the compensation and benefits to which Sample shall be entitled during the period of his consultancy, and thereafter as compensation for any and all accrued benefits vested during his term of employment.

By executing this agreement, except as provided hereinafter, the parties desire to resolve and forever discharge any and all claims, issues, duties, rights, or obligations as now exist or may hereafter arise by reason of the contract with Comco or by reason of any other agreements regarding Sample's employment, whether written or oral.

NOW THEREFORE, in consideration of the covenants and agreements of the parties as set forth herein, it is agreed as follows:

1.   Effective May 1, Sample's employment as Marketing Director for Comco shall be and is hereby terminated for all purposes.

2.   This Agreement shall be deemed effective April 15, 2003. For the period commencing May 1, 2003 and continuing through May 31, 2003 (the "consultancy period"), Sample shall make himself available to the CEO of Comco on a full-time, as-needed basis, during normal working hours, to consult and advise on matters relating to Comco. After May 31, 2003, Sample shall have no further duties to perform for Comco.

3.   During the Consultancy Period, Sample shall receive his current annualized salary, paid in the normal payroll cycle of Comco, and all other current benefits and perquisites pro-vided Sample as Marketing Director.

4.   In consideration of all benefits and rights accrued to Sample by reason of the contract and his service to Comco, including any accrued vacation, sick, or personal leave, Comco hereby agrees to compensate Sample commencing on June 1, 2003 as follows:

(a)   Sample shall receive as compensation for accrued benefits a continuation of his annualized salary at his current rate of pay and in the normal payroll cycle of Comco for a period of eight (8) months beginning June 1, 2003 and ending January 31, 2004.

(b)   During the period of Accrued Benefits Compensation, Comco shall continue to provide Sample med-ical, dental, retirement, and disability benefits currently provided him by Comco (except, in regard to medical, dental, disability, and any other insurance benefits, when Sample receives similar benefits from another employer); and

APPENDICES   205

(c)   Comco shall provide the reasonable cost of defending Sample in the pending litigation known as _____and indemnify Sample on this case and any others arising as a result of his employment.

5.   It is further mutually agreed that neither Comco nor Sample currently have ill will or bad feelings toward the other. Accordingly, it is agreed that Comco will not make any statement that is negative or casts Sample in a bad light; and Sample shall not make any public comment that is negative or casts Comco in a bad light.

This document contains the entire agreement between the parties, may not be amended except by a writing signed by both parties and shall be interpreted in accordance with the laws of the State of Delaware.

IN WITNESS, this document has been executed the day and year first above written.

By: John Sample

By: Thomas Atchison
CEO
Comco

Appendix D

ACKNOWLEDGMENTS

In addition to the publications used for source material and references noted above, I need to give special acknowledgment to a host of reviewers and commenters on the text, including Al Thelen, Bob Turner, Paul Lanspery, Jack Meriwether, Tom Downs, Amy White, Rich Caplan, and Jerry Johnson but none have any responsibility whatsoever for the words finally printed. Recruiters reviewing the text include Bob Murray of Bob Murray and Associates, Norm Roberts of DMG Maximus and Associates, Jerry Oldani of The Oldani Group, and Paul Reaume of PAR, Inc. All the usual disclaimers about lack of responsibility for anything said herein applies to each and all.

I tried to have some fun in dealing with what can be a trying subject. In doing so, I was perhaps swimming upstream. As Tom Corwin is quoted as having said,

"Never make people laugh. If you would succeed in life, you must be solemn. Solemn as an ass. All great monuments are built over solemn asses."

Special acknowledgements go to Ellen Reid of Smarketing, Laren Bright of "Words", Peri Poloni of Knockout Design, Patricia Bacall of Bacall Creative. They helped make the text more readable and the design attractive and relevant.

Appendix E

EXPERIENCE JOHN ARNOLD

When it comes to surviving and prospering in the workplace, John E. Arnold has been there, done that, and written the book on it (which you now hold in your hands). He is engaging, professional, articulate and imminently understandable.

In addition to his books and articles, John makes himself available for speaking engagements to public and private sector enterprises, organizations, and associations and he offers private consultations to individuals.

To engage John's services, contact:

THE John E.
ARNOLD COMPANY
Success and Survival in the 21st Century Workplace

6021 SW 29th St. Suite A #267
Topeka, KS 66614
Phone: 785-228-2143 Toll Free: 1-866-385-1700
Fax: 785-228-2559
Email: info@JohnEArnold.com

or visit

Exurba Publishing, LLC

www.Exurba.com

or

www.JohnEArnold.com

QUICK ORDER FORM

Buy a copy of **Fallback Position** for a friend.

email orders: info@exurba.com

Fax orders: 785-228-2559 Send this form

Telephone orders: Call 1-866-385-1700 toll free

Postal Orders: Exurba Publishing, LLC
                      6021 SW 29th St. Suite A #267
                      Topeka, KS 66614

Please send the following books. I understand I may return any of them for a full refund—for any reason, no questions asked.

_____

_____

_____

_____

Please send more FREE information on :

☐ Other books   ☐ Speaking and Seminars   ☐ Consulting

Name: _____

Address: _____

City_____State_____Zip_____

Telephone: _____

email address:_____

   Sales tax: Please add 6.25% for products shipped to Kansas addresses.

Shipping by air:
US: $4 for the first book and $2 for each additional book.

Payment: ☐ Check   ☐ Credit Card

                  ☐ Visa   ☐ Master Card   ☐ Amex   ☐ Discover

Card Number: _____

Name on Card:_____ Exp. Date ____/____

www.exurba.com